YOUTH
FOOTBALL
SKILLS AND DRILLS

A NEW COACH'S GUIDE

Look for these other coaching guides

Coaching Youth Football: The Baffled Parent's Guide,
by Paul Pasqualoni with Jim McLaughlin

Great Baseball Drills: The Baffled Parent's Guide,
by Jim Garland

Coaching Youth Baseball: The Baffled Parent's Guide,
by Bill Thurston

Great Basketball Drills: The Baffled Parent's Guide,
by Jim Garland

Coaching Youth Basketball: The Baffled Parent's Guide,
by David G. Faucher

Coaching Youth Hockey: The Baffled Parent's Guide,
by Bruce Driver and Claire Wharton

Coaching Boys' Lacrosse: The Baffled Parent's Guide,
by Greg Murrell and Jim Garland

Coaching Girls' Lacrosse: The Baffled Parent's Guide,
by Janine Tucker and Maryalice Yakutchik

Great Soccer Drills: The Baffled Parent's Guide,
by Tom Fleck and Ron Quinn

Coaching Girls' Soccer: The Baffled Parent's Guide
by Drayson Hounsome

Coaching 6-and-Under Soccer: The Baffled Parent's Guide
By David Williams and Scott Graham

Coaching Youth Soccer: The Baffled Parent's Guide,
by Bobby Clark

Coaching Youth Softball: The Baffled Parent's Guide,
by Jacquie Joseph

Coaching Tee Ball: The Baffled Parent's Guide,
by Bing Broido

Teaching Kids Golf: The Baffled Parent's Guide,
by Detty Moore

THE NEW COACH'S GUIDE TO YOUTH FOOTBALL SKILLS AND DRILLS

Tom Bass

Photos by Bruce Curtis

McGraw-Hill

Camden, Maine • New York • Chicago • San Francisco
Lisbon • London • Madrid • Mexico City • Milan
New Delhi • San Juan • Seoul • Singapore • Sydney • Toronto

The McGraw·Hill Companies

1 2 3 4 5 6 7 8 9 DOC D0C 9 8 7 6

Library of Congress Cataloging-in-Publication Data
Bass, Tom.
  Youth football skills and drills : a new coach's guide / Tom Bass.
      p. cm.
  Includes index.
  ISBN 0-07-144179-4 (pbk. : alk. paper)
  1. Youth league football—Coaching—Handbooks, manuals, etc. I. Title.
  GV956.6.B37 2005
  796.332'6—dc22

                                    2005015036

Questions regarding the content of this book should be addressed to
McGraw-Hill/Ragged Mountain Press
P.O. Box 220
Camden, ME 04843

Questions regarding the ordering of this book should be addressed to
The McGraw-Hill Companies
Customer Service Department
P.O. Box 547
Blacklick, OH 43004
Retail customers: 1-800-262-4729
Bookstores: 1-800-722-4726
www.mcgraw-hill.com

I would like to dedicate this book to the thousands of women and men who, every football season, volunteer their time, knowledge and energy to teach young people the skills and techniques needed to play our great game of football.

Contents

Part One: Getting Started

Part Two: Practice

Master Drill List

🕐 Period 1: Warm-Up and Get-on

🕐 Period 2: Individual Practice

🕐 Period 3: Group Practice

⏱ Period 4: Special Teams

⏱ Period 5: Team Practice

⏱ Period 6: Cool-Down and Stretching

Acronyms and Symbols

B

BC – ball carrier
BK – blocker

C

CN – center
CO – corner

D

DB – defensive back
DE – defensive end
DL – defensive lineman
DR – defensive rusher
DT – defensive tackle

F

FB – fullback
FG – field goal
FLK – flanker
FP – force point
FS – free safety

G

GUN – gunner

H

H – holder
HB – halfback

I

IB – inside linebacker
IR – inside rusher

K

K – kicker
KO – kickoff
KR – kick returner

L

LB – linebacker
LDB – left defensive back

LDE – left defensive end
LDT – left defensive tackle
LG – left guard
LGU – left gunner
LIB – left inside linebacker
LN – long snapper
LOB – left outside linebacker
LR – left returner
LT – left tackle
LW – left wing

M

MA – Mac: One of two middle
linebackers in 3 - 4 defense
MB – middle linebacker
MI – Mike: One of two middle
linebackers in 3 - 4 defense

N

NT – nose tackle

O

OB – outside linebacker
OG – offensive guard
OL – offensive lineman
OR – outside rusher
OT – offensive tackle

P

P – punter
PAT – point after touchdown
PB –punt blocker
PK – placekicker
PR – punt returner

Q

QB – quarterback

R

RB – running back
RDB – right defensive back

RDE – right defensive end
RDT – right defensive tackle
RG – right guard
RGU – right gunner
RIB – right inside linebacker
ROB – right outside linebacker
RR – right returner
RT – right tackle
RW – right wing

S
SAF – safety
SB – strong-side linebacker
SE – split end
SN – short snapper
SS – strong safety

T
TB – tailback
TE – tight end
TK – tackler

W
WB – weak-side linebacker
WB – wingback
WR – wide receiver

C	coach
○	offensive player
△	defensive player
⬤	marker
◖	ball
▲	tee
——	run
-----	pass
∿	run with ball
⌐	block
L	step with left foot
R	step with right foot

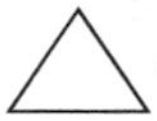

Acknowledgments

A special thanks to my wife Michele for her continuing help on every project; to Bruce Curtis for his excellent photographs; to Rita Rosenkranz my agent on this project; to everyone at McGraw-Hill, especially Ben McCanna, for their encouragement, assistance and dedication to the project; and to Harry Johnston my coaching colleague and friend for reminding me what I was like during my first few years of coaching.

Introduction

Congratulations to you for taking on the responsibility and devoting the time to being a volunteer youth football coach. I hope this book becomes your daily reference guide as you teach young players how to enjoy, understand, and play the game.

In writing this book, my goals were three-fold:

1. To present and explain the basic techniques that young football players must learn to play each position on the team.
2. To provide coaches with drills to teach each of these techniques.
3. To identify the time segment of your practice schedule in which you will best be able to teach and practice each drill.

I want this to be a hands-on football book that will truly help you to instruct youth players and prepare them for the football season.

How to Use This Book

Youth Football Skills and Drills: A New Coach's Guide is divided into two sections. Part I, Getting Started, covers general information to help you begin as a coach. Part II, Practice, focuses on the specific drills and formats to use for each of the periods listed in this general practice schedule:

Period 1	Warm-up and get-on	15 minutes	page 30
Period 2	Individual practice	20 minutes	page 35
Period 3	Group practice	20 minutes	page 156
Period 4	Special teams	10 minutes	page 169
Period 5	Team practice	20 minutes	page 187
Period 6	Cool down and stretching	5 minutes	page 211

This book is designed differently from most technique books in that it is organized according to this practice schedule. The primary goals for each period are explained below, then expanded upon in Chapter 4, Planning the Season.

Periods 1 through 3 focus on starting practice as well as on the specific drills you can use to teach your players the techniques for playing each position on the team.

Many of the drills in Period 2 are unique in that they combine teaching an offensive position with a compatible defensive position. These offensive/defensive combinations help in three ways:

1. They identify which positions a player would play best if he were to play on both offense and defense, something I know many of your players are asked to do.
2. They pair compatible positions, which can be advantageous if you are

faced with a limited coaching staff and your staff must teach both offense and defense.

3. They teach players what an opponent may do in a game to try to defeat them.

Other drills in Period 2 can be used to teach your quarterback the skills he needs to lead your team, to teach tackling and catching—two basic skills every player on your squad must know—and to coordinate the efforts of players in specific positions (for example, a quarterback with running backs or wide receivers, or linebackers with defensive backs). Period 3 covers group practice drills that can be implemented when you work segments of your offense against segments of your defense.

Period 4 has drills for the special teams portion of your daily practice schedule.

Period 5 focuses on working a full offensive team against a full defensive team.

Period 6 deals with cooling the team down and getting them off the field.

Goal Setting

Always try to have a clear picture in your mind of the purpose of each drill. For example, is the drill you are running designed to teach one particular technique that some or all of your players will need to play the game, or is it meant to improve timing or teach assignments to a group of players or to the team?

When the goal of the drill is clear to you, you will be a better teacher, and your young players will not only learn more quickly but also enjoy the process.

For simplicity the book refers to boys, but it should be noted that more and more girls are playing football and moms are taking over coaching duties as well. Both groups of females are making a positive contribution and are a welcome addition to the game.

Getting Started

CHAPTER 1

Becoming a Coach

When you make the decision to become a youth football coach, you take on an enormous responsibility. You are committing yourself to teach young players how to approach the game in a proper manner, provide them with a safe environment in which to play, and impart the life values that come from playing the game.

As a youth coach, you have the opportunity to introduce young players to one of America's greatest games, as well as to enjoy the tremendous personal satisfaction that comes from being a coach.

You will have the chance to see your players grow from a disjointed group of awkward young athletes into a smoothly running team. Initial chaos will be replaced with plays that run like clockwork—and oh, how wonderful the feeling when it starts to click.

First and foremost, you need to be a great teacher. All great coaches are great teachers. As a coach and teacher it will be your responsibility to:

1. Provide a safe and enjoyable setting for learning to take place.

The practical steps for achieving this goal are as follows:

- Inspect the field before the first player arrives for practice.
- Greet each player by name.
- Take a quick check of each player's equipment.
- Preplan the practice so the drills are safe and emphasize proper and safe body movements and positions.
- Be aware of anyone who may be loitering around the field.
- Have at least one coach remain at the field until the last player has been picked up.
- Have a prearranged plan to respond to any medical problem that might occur, including a method of contacting parents.

2. Know what is to be accomplished each day.

You and your coaching staff will want to meet prior to each practice, each meeting, and each game to outline and communicate the goals for that day.

As a coach you need to understand not only what you are going to teach but also how and why it fits into the total team picture. Spend your precious practice time teaching only the particular skills needed for *your* team's offense, defense, or special teams. Should you and your staff determine that the offense will run the ball 70% of the time, try to allocate 70% of your offensive practice time to teaching how to run the ball. On the other hand, if you plan to be a passing team, devote more practice time to perfecting the skills of throwing the ball and running pass routes and less to practicing the skills needed for the option play.

In preparing for a practice, be sure to clarify when you will be teaching an individual technique versus working with the team, and when you will be teaching a skill versus an assignment. For example, when you teach pass protection to the offensive linemen, your concern is how to do the skill. So you need to focus on footwork, balance, and proper positioning of the upper body, lower body, and hands. On the other hand, when you bring the team together to run plays, your focus shifts from teaching *how* to block to teaching *who* to block.

3. Make sure everyone participates and has fun.

Players at all levels, and especially at the youth level, want (and deserve) to participate and have fun in practices and in games. Young players, in particular, want to stay active. Because attention spans may be limited, keep your drills brisk, short, and varied. It is better to use a number of drills to teach one skill than one drill to teach multiple skills.

Example: When you are teaching wide receivers to run a certain pass route, do not use the ball in the drill. Break down the pass route into various drills that can be done quickly by all your receivers. This sequence should include: a stance drill; a start drill in which they drive off the line; a drill in which the focus is on making the break at the correct depth; and, finally, a drill to come out of the break and complete the route.

Design your practices so that you keep all the players active and participating. Multiple repetitions of a short, brisk drill are better than one that goes on forever. Once you have explained the drill, try to keep lectures to a minimum. Above all, keep it fun and upbeat.

4. Present the information in a manner players can understand.

Each coach brings terms and ideas based on his experience and background. Football terms and experiences that are familiar to you may be a foreign language to your players. Make every effort to convey information in a manner they can easily understand. The object is to teach kids, not to impress parents or your peers with your knowledge. When the kids improve and have fun, that's impressive. So:

- Avoid using a one- or two-word term as a shorthand for a skill or technique the first time you teach it. Instead, describe it fully.
- Once you describe it, tell them the name of the skill or technique and use this name each time you refer to it after that.
- Give your players a full description of what you want them to do.
- Have them practice the skill or technique.
- Be prepared that players may need two or three practices to learn football terms; one introduction may not be enough.
- Do the same with drills: teach the drill, give it a name, then refer to the drill only by that name so players equate the drill to the skill being taught.

Example: You may already know in your mind what a "reach block" is and how a player should make this block, but do not assume that your young players have the same knowledge.

5. Be positive when communicating with players, parents, and officials.

As a coach you need to think through what you want your players to do and instruct them in a step-by-step manner, making certain they truly understand what you are asking from them and how it fits into the total football experience. Telling them what *to do* usually takes more thought and may take more time, but your rewards in team performance and the player's improvement will be far greater than when you simply tell them what *not* to do.

Give the same consideration when speaking to a player's parents. Stay positive in your conversation regardless of what the parent is saying to you. Try to answer their questions concerning their son, but avoid being drawn into a discussion of any other player on the team.

Your players will not only learn from what you teach, they will constantly learn by observing your behavior around the team and during a game.

- Treat the least skilled player on the squad exactly as you treat a star player.
- Stay calm.
- Speak respectfully to the team, parents, and officials.
- Show respect in communicating with other staff members.
- Make individual corrections during the game when the player is off the field.
- Be respectful to the opposing coaching staff and team.

One of the greatest lessons your players will learn from you, as a coach, is how you communicate with officials during a game. Show officials the respect they deserve, and save any discussions or questions for a time-out or halftime.

6. Lead so that your players will eagerly follow.

Your players are going to look to you for leadership before, during, and after each practice and game. Their attitudes and conduct will reflect your attitudes and demands. You are their coach, and young players want and expect you to provide:

- Instruction
- Organization
- Structure
- Discipline
- Leadership

Players come to the practice field wanting to learn and have fun. To do so, they need encouragement and positive teaching, and they want you to understand they will make mistakes. In addition, young players want everyone on the team to be treated the same. They do not want stars and whipping boys. They want a team on which everyone is coached with kindness, not ridicule.

Always remember that parents are entrusting you with their most precious possession—their children. Therefore as a coach, it is your responsibility to:

- Treat each child with respect and caring.
- Prepare and teach the skills and rules of the game to your best ability.
- Demonstrate positive life skills, such as good sportsmanship, through your actions and words.
- Allow every child to participate and have fun.

Again, you're to be congratulated on your decision to be a coach. Soon you'll be helping young players learn a great game in a safe and wholesome environment.

CHAPTER 2

Your Coaching Staff

One of the most important keys to success in any football program is the degree to which the members of the coaching staff work together as a unit. Coaches must know and accept their roles on the staff and understand their responsibilities.

Sometimes a first-year coach, full of wonderful ideas and eager to implement them, will find it frustrating when he has to first understand and work with what is already in place. If you're in this position, take the time to appreciate the plan the head coach is implementing before you bring your own ideas forward, and don't be discouraged if your ideas are not immediately added to the program.

It will be easier for the coaching staff to agree on all aspects of coaching the team if they have an opportunity to meet away from the field prior to and during the season. It is during these meetings that each coach's ideas and thoughts may be brought up and discussed, focusing on these broad topics:

- Offensive and defensive scheme and special teams play
- Practice organization
- Game day organization
- Teaching methods
- Individual responsibilities

During these meetings, it is important that everyone be given a chance to speak. The head coach may direct the discussions, but the forum should be open. Once a decision is made, however, everyone on the coaching staff must accept it. At the end of the meeting, the coaches:

- Must be in agreement
- Present a united front
- Speak with one voice

Once on the field, it is important that coaches communicate with players, parents, and one another with a united, respectful voice. The players must receive one message, and this only happens when the coaches are in agreement in every area of coaching. Any disagreements and discussions— and believe me there will be some—are best settled in meetings away from the players and parents.

Every member of the coaching staff must understand and accept the coaching hierarchy of head coach, followed by the offensive and defensive coordinators, then the position coaches. Each coach is important to the successful functioning of the team. The more responsibility a coach has on the staff, the greater will be his input when making a final decision on how the team will be run. Ultimately the head coach has the authority and responsibility to settle any disputes.

For the team to function as one unit, the coaching staff must agree on what to teach as well as how to teach it. As a member of the coaching staff, you must do your part to make this happen.

The ideal coaching staff includes a head coach, an offensive coordinator, a defensive coordinator, a special teams coordinator, and two or three assistant coaches for a total of six or seven staff members. Obviously, the more players you have, the more coaches you need. An ideal ratio would be one coach for every six players. With limited players, teams are forced to have players play both ways—both offense and defense. In this case, coaches can double up and learn to coach on both sides of the ball. Many teams operate with three coaches, with everyone helping in multiple areas. Depending on the number of coaches on staff, each may have more than one role. For example, the head coach often assumes the role of offensive or defensive coordinator and may serve as the special teams coordinator as well. On small staffs, the offensive and defensive line coaches may be the same person. However, for efficiency's sake, one member of the staff should be designated as the coach responsible for the offense, one for the defense, and one for special teams. During a game, each of these areas will need its own coach.

The head coach always has the final say. Each coordinator has the authority for his area of the team during pre-practice planning and actual practices and calls the offensive plays, the defenses, or the special teams plays during the games—but always with the approval and agreement of the head coach.

A position coach has the responsibility of preparing all the players in his position and teaching them the necessary techniques and assignments as charged by the coordinator.

For your team to perform smoothly as one unit, the coaching staff must be coordinated. The key is to clearly define the responsibility of each member of the coaching staff prior to the beginning of the season.

When putting together a coaching staff, and especially one made up of dedicated volunteers, the first thing to be done as a staff is to decide on common goals and agree on the method and manner of coaching the team.

These include the following:

- Practice schedule and tempo of practice
- Techniques to be taught
- Offensive, defensive, and special teams schemes to be taught
- Game day organization and responsibilities
- How to address discipline problems

It is great when all members of the coaching staff agree, but if there is a difference of opinion, the head coach must step in and set the policy. It is also critical that each coach's unique strengths be identified and fully utilized, and this is much more than focusing on who has played a certain position in the past or whose son is playing that position now. Pro Football Hall of Fame Coach Paul Brown once told me, "If you surround yourself with people just like you, your players will be cheated."

It is important to find one area that each coach has a special interest in or does better than any other coach on the staff, then give him that responsibility. For example, an individual coach may have:

- A real interest in physical fitness and be more than willing to lead the team in the warm-up, cool-down, and stretching exercises
- An interest in setting up and facilitating an e-mail and communications network for the entire team
- Organizational skills and can provide team schedules, practice plans, game plans, Excel depth charts, and testing records
- The ability to design and produce your offensive, defensive, and special teams plays for your playbook
- Special game-day abilities that allow him to recognize what your opponent is doing and provide suggestions to improve the team's performance
- Special first-aid and Red Cross training in case of an injury on the field

The coaching staff must set aside time to review the rules of the game and to establish an agreed upon policy and procedure for discussions with parents concerning their child's position or playing time with the team. Coaches must listen respectfully to parents, understand their concerns, and assure them that those concerns will be communicated to the entire coaching staff. Again, be sure to avoid speaking about the ability of another player when having a discussion with parents.

Before the team can come together, the players need to see the coaches cooperating, speaking with one voice, working toward the same goals, and performing as one cohesive unit.

Player Positions

It is important for each coach to know all the positions on the team and to develop a fundamental understanding of what is required to play each position. Because terminology will differ from team to team and coach to coach, the staff should agree on the names for the positions and what each position can be expected to contribute to the team's success.

Given the limited number of players on many youth teams, it is often necessary for kids to "play both ways." At the end of this chapter I offer a proposed scheme of complementary offensive and defensive positions for young players.

Offensive Positions and Responsibilities

Offensive Line—Five Players

The offensive line is made up of five players: two offensive tackles (OT), two offensive guards (OG) and one center (CN).

On running plays, the five offensive linemen:

1. Stop the defensive man's charge (*neutralize*).
2. Push and turn the defensive man off the line of scrimmage (*block*).
3. Create a space for the ball carrier to run (*open a hole or running lane*).

On passing plays, the offensive linemen:

1. Form an area for the quarterback to throw (*set the pocket*).
2. Keep the defensive man from reaching the quarterback (*pass protect*).

TB/HB
FB
QB
FLK/WB
TE OT OG CN OG OT SE

The center has the additional and important responsibility of handing the ball to the quarterback to start every play (*making the snap*).

When selecting offensive linemen, look for players who have the following traits:

- Good strength
- Good balance
- Quickness for a short distance—not necessarily 40 yards

Receiving Corps—Three Players

The receiving corps is usually made up of three players: one tight end (TE) and two wide receivers—the flanker and split end (FLK and SE). When the flanker lines up just outside the tight end's position, he will usually be referred to as a wingback (WB) and may be counted as part of the offensive backfield.

On running plays:

- The flanker and split end will block defensive backs (DB)—either a safety (SS or FS) or a corner (CO)—(*block downfield*)
- The tight end will push or turn a linebacker (LB) or defensive end (DE) off the line of scrimmage (*block*)

On passing plays the wide receivers and tight end will:

1. Sprint off the line of scrimmage (*release*).
2. Run to a specific area of the field (*run a pattern*).
3. Separate from the defensive man (*get open*).
4. Catch the pass from the quarterback (*completion*).

When selecting your receiving corps, look for players with these traits:

- Smaller players with speed, agility, and good hand-eye coordination to be your wide receivers
- A player with strength, balance, and speed to be your tight end
- Good hands and a determination to catch the ball in all three receivers

Offensive Backfield—Three Players

The offensive backfield is normally made up of three players: the quarterback (QB), a fullback (FB), and one running back (RB). If the running back lines up directly behind the quarterback, he is often called the tailback (TB). If he lines up behind an offensive tackle, he is commonly called the halfback (HB). If the flanker lines up just outside the tight end's position, he is usually referred to as a wingback (WB) and may be counted as part of the offensive backfield.

On running plays, the quarterback must:

1. Get the ball from the center (CN) (*take the snap*).

2. Give or pitch the ball (*handoff*) to a halfback/tailback (HB/TB) or fullback (FB) (*ball carrier*).
3. Fake setting up to pass (*play action pass*).

The halfback/tailback usually carries the ball, though he may also be asked to block when the fullback carries the ball. The fullback usually precedes the ball carrier and blocks defensive players (*lead blocker*).

On passing plays, the quarterback must:

1. Take the ball from the center and sprint away from the line of scrimmage (*drop back*).
2. Set up to throw behind the offensive line (*in the pocket*).
3. Throw the ball to the open receiver (*pass*).

On passing plays, the halfback will either:

- Be one of the receivers and go out for a pass (*run a pass route*)
- Block a linebacker if he rushes the quarterback (*pass protect*)

On passing plays, the fullback will usually be asked to either:

- Stay in and help the offensive line block for the quarterback (*pass protect*)
- Run a delayed pass route if there is no one to block (*safety valve*)

When selecting players for your offensive backfield, look for these qualities:

- The quarterback should be smart, agile, and able to pass the ball accurately
- The halfback/tailback must have speed, quickness, and be able to change direction (*cut*). He should also be able to catch the ball and have the mental toughness to want to carry and protect the ball
- The fullback needs to be strong, be a good blocker, and run with power

Defensive Positions and Responsibilities

Defensive Line—Four Players

Usually the defensive line comprises four players: two defensive tackles (DT) and two defensive ends (DE). Although many teams have up to five or six defensive linemen, some teams play with only three. If one of the defensive tackles lines up directly in front of the offensive center, he is referred to as a nose tackle (NT).

On running plays, the defensive linemen are charged with:

1. Stopping the offensive blocker (*neutralize*).
2. Getting rid of the blocker (*shedding the block*).
3. Locating and moving to the ball carrier and making the tackle (*pursuit*).

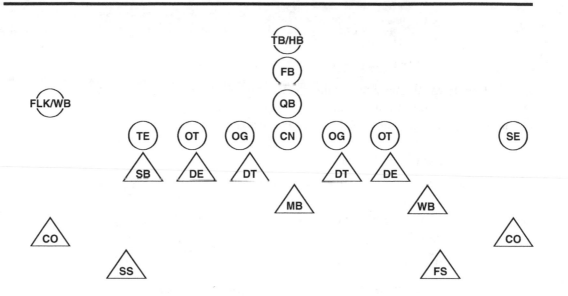

On passing plays, defensive linemen are charged with:

1. Rushing at the quarterback (*pass rush*).
2. Putting their hands up to hit the ball (*getting a deflection*).
3. Tackling the quarterback before he can throw the ball (*getting a sack*).

When selecting defensive linemen, look for players who have the following traits:

• Good strength, especially in the legs, upper body, arms, and shoulders
• Quickness over short distances (*burst*)
• Quick reactions to the ball being centered (*going on the snap*)

Linebackers—Three Players

The defensive linebackers include three players: two outside backers—a "strong-side" backer (SB) who lines up on the same side as the tight end and a "weak-side" backer (WB) who lines up on the opposite side—plus a middle backer (MB) who lines up in front of the offensive center. Defenses may play with more or fewer than the three linebackers shown here.

On running plays, the linebackers are charged with:

1. Moving up to the line of scrimmage (*attacking the line*).
2. Stopping the offensive blocker (*neutralize*).
3. Getting rid of the blocker (*shedding the block*).
4. Turning the ball carrier back to the inside of the field (*contain*).
5. Locating and moving to the ball carrier and making the tackle (*pursuit*).

On passing plays, the linebackers' jobs vary. They may be asked to do any of the following:

- Run (*rush*) at the quarterback (*blitz*)
- Run with a receiver (*cover*), usually a back, all over the field (*man-to-man coverage*)
- Sprint to a designated area of the field (*drop*) and react when the ball is thrown (*zone coverage*)

When selecting linebackers, look for players who are:

- Smart and love to play the game
- Strong, especially in the upper body
- Blessed with good speed and quickness
- Good tacklers with a desire to make the tackle (*nose for the ball*)

Defensive Backfield—Four Players

The defensive backfield is made up of four players: two corners (CO), who line up opposite the wide receivers, and two safeties—a strong safety (SS) who lines up on the side of the tight end and a free safety (FS) who lines up in front of the ball or on the side opposite the tight end. Some defenses may only use three defensive backs.

On running plays, the defensive backs must:

1. Make certain that it is truly a run (*read the play*).
2. Come up to the line if they can and if it is their responsibility (*force*).
3. Locate and get rid of any blocker (*shed the block*).
4. Turn the ball carrier back to the center of the field (*contain*).
5. Move to the ball carrier and help make the tackle (*pursuit*).

On passing plays, the defensive backs can have several roles:

- Sprint to a designated area of the field (*drop*) and react when the ball is thrown (*zone coverage*)
- Run with a receiver (*cover*), usually the tight end and wide receivers, all over the field (*man-to-man coverage*)
- Prevent the offensive player from making the catch (*break up*)
- Occasionally run at the quarterback (*blitz*)
- Attempt to make the catch (*interception*)

When selecting defensive backs, look for players who:

- Have great speed
- Are smart
- Quickly put mistakes behind them during the game
- Compete on every play
- Are good tacklers and willing to tackle any ball carrier or receiver
- Have good hands to make an interception

Complementary Positions for Players Going Both Ways

With limited players on a squad, many players will be required to learn to play both an offensive and defensive position (*going both ways*) during a game. By assigning complementary positions the players can use the knowledge learned from one side of the ball (offense or defense) to their advantage when lining up on the opposite side of the ball.

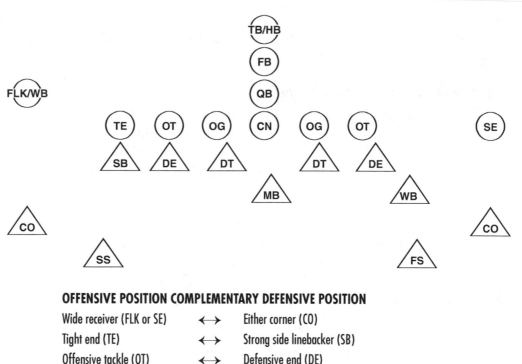

OFFENSIVE POSITION COMPLEMENTARY DEFENSIVE POSITION

OFFENSIVE POSITION		COMPLEMENTARY DEFENSIVE POSITION
Wide receiver (FLK or SE)	←→	Either corner (CO)
Tight end (TE)	←→	Strong side linebacker (SB)
Offensive tackle (OT)	←→	Defensive end (DE)
Offensive guard (OG)	←→	Defensive tackle (DT)
Center (CN)	←→	Middle linebacker (MB)
Fullback (FB)	←→	Weak side linebacker (WB)
Quarterback (QB)	←→	Free safety (FS)
Tailback/halfback (TB/HB)	←→	Strong safety/corner (SS/CO)

There is great carryover value, and learning seems to be easier, when players assume a defensive position that is directly across the ball from their offensive alignment. For example, it is often easier for a defensive lineman to learn how to recognize and defeat a certain block if he has learned how to make that block while playing on the offensive side of the ball. A defensive corner will recognize a pass route and react to it quicker when he has learned how to properly run the route when playing as a wide receiver.

You may not always be able to match an offensive player's position with a complementary position on defense, but when you can, you and the player will usually be happy with the results.

Special Teams

When your team is involved in any segment of a kicking game (i.e., special teams), use a combination of offensive and defensive players. In fact, when thinking about special teams, think in terms of two teams rather than one in your planning. After all, when one team is making a kick, there will always be a corresponding team lined up on the other side of the ball.

Special teams require some very specialized jobs to be filled.

CORRESPONDING KICKING TEAMS

Point after touchdown/field goal	←→	Field goal block
Kickoff	←→	Kickoff return
Punt	←→	Punt return/punt rush

Each segment of a kicking game features one or more players who will need to have special skills to succeed.

Point after Touchdown and Field Goal—Three Players

For your point after touchdown/field goal (PAT/FG) team, you need three specialized players: a center who is designated as a short snapper (SN), a holder (H), and a placekicker (PK).

When attempting to kick a PAT or FG, the short snapper, usually a lineman or linebacker, must complete the following:

1. Line up in the center position.
2. Throw the ball back between his legs 7 yards to the holder (*short snap*).
3. Help block the opposing players who are trying to block the kick.

The holder, usually a quarterback or wide receiver, has these responsibilities:

1. Kneel down 7 yards behind the center and establish the spot for the ball.
2. Signal the center that the kicker is ready.
3. Catch the ball from the center (*take the snap*).

Then the holder has to either:

• Place the ball on the ground (*on the spot*) and balance the ball on its point for the placekicker
• Run or pass the ball if there is a bad snap (*fire play*)

The placekicker, who can play any position on the team, has to:

1. Line up properly.
2. Signal the holder that he is ready to make the kick.
3. Take the correct steps and kick the ball.

It is essential that these three players practice together as a unit until each player can do his own job satisfactorily. When selecting players for your PAT/FG team kicking unit:

- The short snapper must be able to accurately throw the ball back 7 yards to the holder and have the bulk to aid in the blocking
- The holder must have good hands to be able to catch the snap and place it correctly on the ground plus have the ability to run or pass the ball
- The placekicker should have a strong leg and be able to kick the ball off the ground from a hold through the uprights and over the crossbar

The field goal block team should be made up of players from your normal defensive team.

Kickoff Team—One Player

For your kickoff team, you only need one specialized player: the kicker (K). When kicking off, the kicker, who can play any position on the team, must complete the following:

1. Place the ball on the tee.
2. Line up properly for the kick.
3. Signal his teammates that he is ready to make the kick.
4. Take the correct steps and kick the ball.
5. Be in position to make a tackle if necessary (*play safety*).

A kicker should have a strong leg and be able kick the ball off the tee to the left, center, and right areas of the field. The remaining ten members of the kickoff team should have good speed and desire to cover the kick, stop the return, and also be good tacklers.

The kickoff return team should be made up of nine players who have the agility and ability to block while they are running, and two players who can catch the kickoff and run the ball back up the field (kick returner). The latter two players may be running backs, wide receivers, or defensive backs.

Punt Team—Two Players

You need two specialized players for your punt team: a center who is designated as a long snapper (LN) and a punter (P).

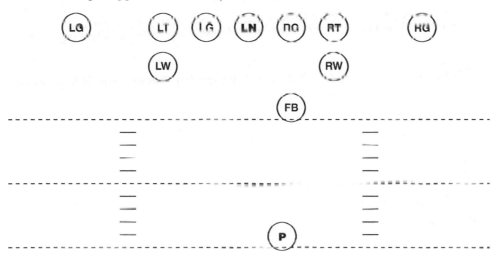

When attempting to kick a punt, the long snapper, usually a lineman or linebacker, must:

1. Line up in the center position.
2. Throw the ball back between his legs 10–13 yards to the punter (*long snap*).
3. Help block opposing players who are trying to block the kick.
4. Run down the field after the kick to help tackle any return man (*cover*).

The punter, who can play any position on the team, must:

1. Line up at the correct distance from the long snapper.
2. Signal the fullback (FB) that he is ready to make the punt.
3. Catch the ball from the center (*take the snap*).
4. Take the correct steps and kick the ball.
5. Punt the ball to the desired area of the field.
6. Be in position to make a tackle if necessary (*play safety*).

It is essential that these two players practice together as a two-man unit until each player can do his job satisfactorily.

Look for these traits when you are selecting players for your punt team kicking unit:

- The long snapper must be able to accurately throw the ball back 10–13 yards to the punter, have the bulk to aid in the blocking, and have enough speed and agility to run downfield and tackle the return man
- The punter should have good hands to catch the snap, a strong leg to make the kick, and the ability to punt the ball correctly

The remaining nine players on the punt team can come from your offensive and defensive teams. The two outside men, called gunners (LG/RG), need to be the fastest men on the punt team and will usually be defensive backs or wide receivers. The fullback (FB) may be a fullback, halfback, or linebacker and needs to be the leader of the punt team.

The punt return team should be made up of nine players who have the agility and ability to rush the punter and block while running, and two players who can catch the punt and run the ball back up the field (kick returner). These two players may be running backs, wide receivers, or defensive backs.

Every player on your team should have one or more positions on your special teams. Since one-fourth to one-third of all your plays during a game will be some form of special teams, it is important that you devote the proportional team practice time and additional time to players who have a specialized position. Field position can be gained or lost and close games won by special teams play.

Planning the Season

One of the first things any coach recognizes is that there never seems to be enough time to practice everything you want to cover. Thus, early on, you need to establish priorities for how you will conduct the practices and how much time you will allocate for each segment of practice.

I have always found it helpful to break the practice down into the six segments mentioned in the Introduction:

Period 1	Warm-up and get-on	15 minutes
Period 2	Individual practice	20 minutes
Period 3	Group practice	20 minutes
Period 4	Special teams	10 minutes
Period 5	Team practice	20 minutes
Period 6	Cool-down and stretching	5 minutes

Each period should accomplish a particular goal or goals; teaching individual skills, techniques to be used versus an opponent, or assignments for offensive plays, defenses, or special teams.

You can adjust the length of each period up or down to fit your needs for the week and the time constraints faced by your team. For example, early in the year you may find it necessary to spend more time on individual practice as you teach the various techniques and skills needed to play each position. Then as the year progresses, you may decide to cut down the group practice period and lengthen your team practice period accordingly.

As a youth coach, you may face the added challenge of having a limited number of players, requiring players to play both offense and defense. This may mean you will need to designate one day's practice as an offensive day and the next as a defensive day. Telling your players ahead of time what segment of the game is the day's priority will help them be comfortable and organized during the practice.

Schedule Breakdown

Period 1—Warm-Up and Get-On

Gather the entire team into predetermined rows by positions. As youth coach, your goal for this period is to increase the core temperature of your players by having them jog four times across the field in groups at the start of practice. If you are practicing on a field that is not marked, have your players jog from one coach to another for a predetermined distance, using cones. This type of setup will also instantly tell you if a player is absent from practice. For the get-on segment of this period, you can introduce a new offensive or defensive play depending on the focus of the day. It should be short and to the point.

Period 2—Individual Practice

Divide the team into the various segments of the football team so you can teach the techniques needed for playing each position. The actual number of groups will depend on the number of coaches on your staff and the phase of the game being emphasized that day. Drills in this period should be short in duration, teach a particular technique, and provide for the maximum number of repetitions.

Period 3—Group Practice

This period gives you the opportunity to work various groups of players against one another. The amount of time needed and the drills you use will vary from one practice to the next but can include passing drills in which the receivers run their routes against the coverage of the defensive backs, and the offensive line practices pass protection against the defensive linemen's pass rush. It can also be used to work on half-line drills versus half defenses. This period should focus on techniques in the one-on-one drills and assignments in the half-line drills.

Period 4—Special Teams

In this period you have the opportunity to focus on one or more of the special teams segments that you will need for a game, especially when they correspond to one another. As an example, it may be possible to work with the punt team and punt return team at the same time if you have the available coaches and players.

Period 5—Team Practice

During team practice, you can work the entire offense against the entire defense. One side should service the other based on the day's focus. For example, on an offensive day, the defense provides a picture for the offense and practices at a tempo set by the offensive coaches. On defensive day, the opposite occurs, with the offense running the plays needed by the defense at the tempo set by the defensive coaches. Here the major focus is on assignments and working as a unit. This should be a learning period with full scrimmages held to a minimum.

Period 6—Cool-Down and Stretching

This period should be a time for the team to come together and run either offensive plays or defenses "against the air," running a set distance every play. Use this period for conditioning, but keep the focus football-oriented.

Get Organized

I believe that it is very important to start practice as a team and to end as a team. Try not to end with some players leaving practice while others are still on the field.

Look at the practice schedule and determine what you want to accomplish during each time period. Your daily practice sessions may change as the year progresses. You may find that you need to shorten or lengthen a period based on the challenges presented by an upcoming opponent.

It is important for the coaching staff to.

- Keep the practice routine as consistent as possible
- Be organized in its approach
- Tell players at the beginning of practice what the practice will include
- Agree to stick to the practice times to avoid holding up the rest of the team

Practice

Part II provides the hands-on elements that will help you teach players the techniques, skills, and assignments of football. In Period 1 we look at warm-up drills; then, in Period 2, we show you how to make best use of the segment of your practice devoted to individual skills and techniques for the various positions. In this critical segment, the coaching staff teaches the techniques players need to master. It is during this period that you will see your players improve. It is wonderful when suddenly the light goes on, and they grasp what you are trying to teach!

Periods 3, 4, and 5 focus on drills that can be used when working the offense versus the defense either in group work or as a full team.

Finally, Period 6 features the final segment of your practice where you cool the players down prior to leaving the field.

It is important to fight the tendency to eliminate the period for individual practice as the year goes along. Maintaining and reinforcing proper technique contribute to each player's ongoing improvement and increases the team's opportunities for winning games.

During your individual period, follow these guidelines as you prepare to instruct your players:

1. Determine the exact techniques your players will need to play each position.
2. Think through how you will tell a player what you want him "to do"; avoid telling him what "not to do."
3. Design a separate drill for each technique.
4. Take the time to explain the drill completely at the beginning of the year.
5. Name each drill so the players know immediately how to line up and what is expected of them when you call out the name of the drill.
6. Run a larger number of short, quick drills rather than a small number of long drills.
7. Keep instruction to a minimum and movement to a maximum.
8. Focus on multiple repetitions before moving on to another drill.
9. Design drills to use every day and also as part of your pregame warm-up activity.

The number of position groups you can break out to will be determined by the number of coaches on your staff. Ideally you want three coaches on defense (defensive backs, linebackers, defensive line) and four coaches on offense (running backs, receivers, quarterback, offensive line). This allows you to have a coach for each position and offers the flexibility to work on both offense and defense in each practice by splitting into seven groups for each individual period.

With a smaller staff it may be necessary to combine groups and work on offensive techniques one day and defensive techniques another. With this setup, the offensive and defensive line could be under one coach, the wide receivers, quarterbacks, and defensive backs under another coach, and the running backs and linebackers under a third coach.

The latter configuration is not the best, but it does force your players to learn the techniques needed to play on both offense and defense, something they may be called upon to do in a game.

The drills may be specific for one segment of the team or can be used by two or more positions individually or in combination. Drills in which two or more positions on one side of the ball work together are called combination drills. The appropriate positions are listed with the drill.

One of the challenges you may face is practicing on a field that is not lined in a football configuration. If this is your situation, it is good to have heavy string or light rope cut into lengths of 20 yards, with a marking every yard, that can be used to set out distance markers for your various drills. This method gives you an accurate measurement, your players a point of reference, and establishes a line of scrimmage for the team.

The drills in the following chapters are grouped using opposing positions and designed with the thought that a player may be asked to go both ways—offense and defense—playing two positions on the team.

PERIOD 1
Warm-Up and Get-On

Warm-Up Drills

In recent years, there has been a great deal of research on the benefits of pre-practice warm-up activities, especially for youth teams. Although basic stretching for the big muscle groups, especially the legs, is still advisable, elaborate pre-practice stretching has slowly been replaced by an emphasis on conducting movements that will increase the core body temperature of each player before the practice begins.

You can increase your players' core temperatures by having them jog four times across the field in groups at the start of the practice. Have them jog from one coach to another for a predetermined distance, or use cones, if you're practicing on an unmarked field.

Ideally, your warm-up will:

- Use the same movements at every practice (and pregame warm-ups) so your players can begin each time without instruction
- Ensure that each player's core temperature is brought up

You may want to divide your team into groups, as in the following scheme:

- Quarterbacks, running backs, and wide receivers
- Offensive linemen, tight ends, and special teams specialists
- Defensive linemen (DL) and middle linebackers
- Outside backers (OBs) and defensive backs

However, if you have players who play on both sides of the ball, this scheme may not be the most efficient way to divide your squad. Adjust as necessary by running drills on defensive alignment one day and offensive alignment the next for any two-way players.

🏈 JOG

Number of players: All players
Equipment: Shorts or full pads
Time: 3 minutes/each day

| C | | | | | | | | | | | | | | | C |

C (WR)(WR)(WR)(WR)(RB)(RB)(RB)(QB)(QB)(QB)(RB)(RB)(RB)(WR)(WR)(WR) C

(OL)(OL)(OL)(OL)(OL)(OL)(OL)(OL)(TE)(TE)(K)(P)

(DL)(DL)(DL)(DL)(MB)(MB)(MB)(DL)(DL)(DL)(DL)

(DB)(DB)(DB)(DB)(OB)(OB)(OB)(OB)(DB)(DB)(DB)(DB)

1. Divide the players into groups. Players in the first group move up to the line and get into a comfortable stance.

2. A coach blows a whistle or gives the command of "Hut," signaling the group to jog down the field to the other coaches.
3. The next group immediately steps up to the line and gets in position to go.
4. The coach signals the next group to start when the preceding group is 10 yards downfield.
5. Each group runs 4 laps during the drill.

Coaching Points

- Run one group at a time.
- Do not start a group until every player in the group is set at the line.
- Encourage the players to jog, not sprint, during their run.

After the Jog drill, move immediately into the Start drill.

 START

Number of players: All players
Equipment: Shorts or full pads
Time: 4 minutes/each day

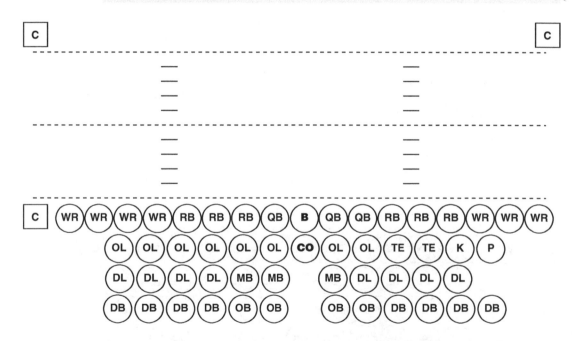

In this drill, shorten the running distance to 10 yards. Start your players from the stance that you will have them use in the game. For example, the quarterback should take the stance that he will use to get the snap from the center. If your tailback uses a 2-point stance, he should take that stance for the drill. The same will hold true for all the other positions on the team. Try to have these movements mirror what each player will be asked to do in a game.

1. Divide the players into groups. Players in the first group move up to the line and get into the stance they will use in a game.
2. A coach gives the command of "Hut" for the offensive groups or "Move the ball" for the defensive players.
3. The group runs 10 yards, then peels around to the outside and returns to the starting line.
4. The next group immediately steps up to the line and gets in position.
5. Players should run their 10 yards at near full speed.
6. Each group runs four repetitions: 1) straight ahead or straight back, 2) starting to the right, 3) starting to the left, and 4) straight ahead or back.

Coaching Points

- Run one group at a time.
- Do not start a group until every player in the group is set at the line.
- Make certain that no player is offside during the drill. If one player is offside, make the entire group run again.
- When moving forward, check that the players are stepping forward with their first step and not taking a step back to get started.
- When moving to their right or left, OBs should cross over the foot that's in the direction they want to go. The other offensive players should take a directional step with the foot on the side of their movement.
- Instruct defensive linemen to take either a directional step or a crossover step when going to their right or left.
- Have MBs and OBs shuffle when going right or left.
- Instruct defensive backs to turn around to get into their stance so they can run backward during the entire drill, angling to their right or left but remaining in their backpedal.
- Check that the players are running hard for the entire 10 yards.

Get-On

While the warm-up phase of Period 1 gets the players' bodies ready for practice, the get-on phase gets them thinking about the game. For the remainder of Period 1, you can quickly introduce and run 1) one or two new offensive plays, 2) one or two new defenses or opponent's plays, or 3) a phase of special teams (punt/punt return, kickoff/kickoff return, PAT/FG, PAT/FG block, onside kick/hands team). Be sure to tell your players what you plan to work on, so that they know what is being taught and which phase of the game they should focus on.

Introduce the plays as quickly as possible, then have the players run them at a brisk pace. Total time for this phase of Period 1 should be no more than five to six minutes.

Focus on teaching the players their assignments for the new material and do not worry about proper technique at this time.

Get-On

- Set up full offensive and defensive teams.
- Based on the new material (offense or defense), tell each player what his assignment will be.
- Allow them to walk through the offensive or defensive play.
- Line up the opposing players on one knee as there should not be any contact.
- Run the play at half speed.
- Rotate the players so that every player has a chance to practice the new material.
- Expect mistakes and remember this is only an introductory period.

PERIOD 2
Individual Practice

Defensive Back and Wide Receiver Drills

Defensive Back Drills

Many young players find that playing defensive back is a challenge because they must learn to run backwards just as fast as their opponent is running forward. It takes time for a defensive back to become comfortable running backwards. Pay close attention to each player's technique and be sure to repeatedly practice each drill so that running backwards becomes second nature.

 **STANCE**

Number of players: All defensive backs (corner, free safety, strong safety)
Equipment: Shorts or full pads
Time: 2 minutes/every day

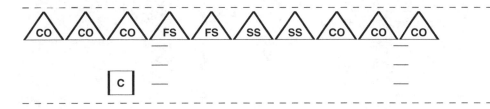

1. All the defensive backs line up across the field facing the coach.
2. On the command "Stance," each player gets into his proper stance (see below).

3. The coach scans down the line and checks that everyone is properly set.

4. On the command of "Up," the players come out of their stance to an upright position.

Coaching Points

- In the beginning of the year, go one player at a time until you are confident that each player understands how to start correctly.
- For the CO stance:
    1. The CO steps forward and in with his outside foot, turning the foot to the inside so that it is directly under his nose.
    2. The majority of his weight is on the outside edge of this front foot, allowing him to use the muscles of the lower leg to push back when he starts.
    3. His knees are bent, back straight, head up and looking in, shoulders forward, and arms hanging down in a comfortable manner.
    4. Check that the CO's weight is on the front foot by asking him to lift his back foot.
- COs may be uncomfortable when first getting into their stance, but they will soon see that it gives them a greater push in their start.
- You may want to teach all your defensive backs to line up in a corner stance if you feel they may have to play corner during the year.
- For the SS stance:
    1. The SS assumes a similar stance as CO except that his front foot comes straight forward, thus assuming a more balanced stance.

DB Stance

Strong safety stance. (left)

Free safety stance. (right)

- For the FS stance:
  1. The FS stands upright with his feet even, shoulder-width apart.
  2. His shoulders are forward and arms hanging in a relaxed fashion.

START

Number of players: All DBs
Equipment: Shorts or full pads
Time: 2 minutes/every day

DB Start

<!-- Diagram: row of triangles labeled CO CO CO FS FS SS SS CO CO CO, with box labeled C below -->

1. All the defensive backs line up across the field facing the coach.
2. On the command of "Stance," each player gets into his proper stance (see Stance drill above).
3. The coach scans down the line and checks that everyone is properly set.
4. On the command of "Hut," each player makes his start by taking two or three steps straight back.
5. After making their start, the players line up again and repeat the drill.

Coaching Points

- In the beginning of the year, go one player at a time until you are confident that each player understands how to start correctly.
- In making their start:
  1. The COs usually have a WR coming at them on the snap of the ball, so it is important for them to push off with the front foot, projecting their hips back, and taking a step back with their back foot.
  2. The SS should also try to push off his front foot and step back with his back foot, although it will not be as far a step as the CO may take.
  3. The FS usually takes a very short step back with either foot.
- With their first step, all players should step back and not forward to get started.

🏈 BACKPEDAL

Number of players: All DBs
Equipment: Shorts or full pads, markers
Time: 2 minutes/every day

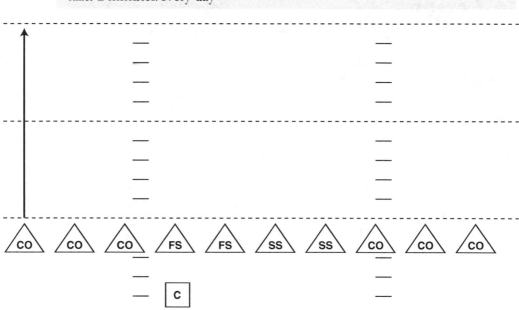

1. All the defensive backs line up, spread out across the field facing the coach.
2. On the command of "Stance," each player gets into his proper stance (see Stance drill).
3. The coach scans down the line and checks that everyone is properly set.
4. On the command of "Hut," each player starts and runs backwards for 10 yards.
5. The players line up again and repeat the drill.

Coaching Points

- In the beginning of the year, go one player at a time until you are confident that each player understands how to start correctly.
- To Backpedal, players:
  1. Step backward with each step.
  2. Have their shoulders in front of their hips, their heads up, and their arms moving in a natural running motion.

FORWARD RUN

Number of players: All DBs
Equipment: Shorts or full pads
Time: 3 minutes/every day

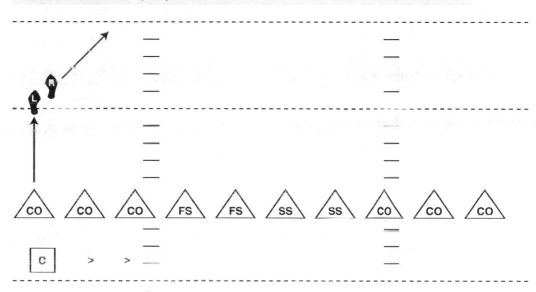

1. All the defensive backs line up, spread out across the field facing the coach.
2. On the command of "Stance," each player gets into his proper stance (see Stance drill).
3. On the command of "Hut," each player starts and runs straight back for 5 yards.
4. When the player nears 5 yards, the coach points deep to the right or left indicating the direction in which the player is to turn and go to a forward run.
5. The player continues his forward run for 5 yards before returning to his starting spot.

Coaching Points

- Have players go one at a time, moving down the line.
- For a Forward Run, the player:
    1. Leans his upper body in the direction he plans to go.
    2. Brings the opposite leg across his body in a natural motion.
    3. Keeps his feet under his hips as he runs and maintains his momentum throughout the drill. This will keep him from slipping on a wet surface or stopping and starting again when he goes into his forward run.
- Be sure each player has the chance to go deep to his right and left.

Helping to Stop the Run

The previous defensive back drills have focused on teaching techniques that can be used in pass defense. There will be times during the game when a defensive back will be required to come up and become part of the defense against an offensive running play. This action (*run force*) may be used by either the corner or safety. Normally the defensive back will be coming from the outside.

🏈 RUN FORCE

Number of players: 6 players
Equipment: Full pads, markers
Time: 5 minutes/once a week

1. In this drill, the extra FS can be the ball carrier (BC), an extra CO can be the blocker (BK), and an extra SS can line up as the TE and LB.
2. Prior to the start of the drill, the coach indicates which defensive back has responsibility for forcing the run.
3. The coach calls out "Ready" and "Hut," which starts the drill.
4. On "Hut," the TE steps in to the player lined up as the LB. The BK and BC start to their right.
5. The designated defensive back immediately heads for a spot 3 yards outside the TE's block and 2 yards across the line of scrimmage—the force point (FP).
6. The defensive back meets the BK at the force point with his inside shoulder turning the BC back to the inside to the LB's position.

Coaching Points

- Teach the defensive back who is forcing the run to keep his outside arm and leg free in case the BC tries to go to the outside.
- Once the defensive backs are coming up properly, have the three offensive players huddle up and every three or four plays have the TE release downfield for a pass instead of blocking.
- If the designated defensive back charges up and does not start back when the TE releases up the field, you will know he is not focused on the TE at the start of each play.
- Give each defensive player a chance to read the TE's block, attack the force point, and force the BC to the inside.
- Alternate running the drill to the right and to the left.
- Always start this drill with everyone going half speed.

Wide Receiver Drills

There are basic drills for wide receivers (WRs) that do not include the quarterback or the ball. Once the ball comes into the drill, the focus shifts to reception, and often the details of running the pattern are lost.

2-POINT STANCE

Number of players: All WRs
Equipment: Shorts or full pads
Time: 2 minutes/every day

1. All wide receivers line up across the field facing the coach.
2. On the command of "Stance," each player gets into his proper stance (see below).
3. The coach scans down the line and checks that everyone is properly set.
4. On the command of "Up," the players come out of their stance to an upright position.

Coaching Points

- In the beginning of the year, go one player at a time until you are confident that each player understands how to start correctly.

WR 2-Point Stance

Wide receiver stance.

- For a 2-Point Stance:
1. The wide receiver stands upright, with his feet even and spread hip width.
2. On the command of "Stance," he steps forward with his outside foot so the heel of the forward foot is ahead of the toe of the back foot. The majority of his weight is on the forward foot.
3. The knees are slightly flexed, shoulders and head are leaning forward ahead of the hips, and the back is straight.
4. The arms and hands are relaxed and hanging down, and his head is turned in to see the ball.

START

Number of players: All WRs
Equipment: Shorts or full pads, markers
Time: 2 minutes/every day

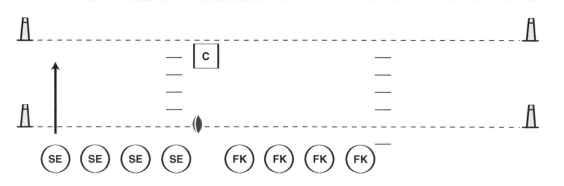

1. All wide receivers line up across the field and face the coach.
2. On the command of "Stance," each player gets into his proper 2-point stance.
3. The coach scans down the line and checks that everyone is properly set.
4. On the command of "Hut," each player takes two or three steps forward.
5. After making their start (see below), the players line up again and repeat the drill.

Coaching Points

- In the beginning of the year, go one player at a time until you are confident that each player understands how to start correctly.
- Making the Start:
  1. The receiver stands upright, with his feet even and spread hip-width and then moves his outside foot up for the proper stance.
  2. As the receiver starts, he rolls his weight forward over the ball of his front foot and at the same time takes a forward step with his back foot. He should not take a false step backward with his front foot, as this will slow him down.
  3. He keeps leaning forward, gaining ground with each step, and swinging his arms in a normal running action.
  4. His head and eyes look forward so that in a game he can see the defensive backs.

Learning the Basic Pass Routes

In the following wide receiver drills, we work on the basic pass routes (or pass patterns) that you may use in your passing attack. The patterns you feature will depend on the passing ability of your quarterback, the ability of your offensive line to pass protect, and the catching ability of your wide receivers. Spend a majority of your time in practice throwing the passes you feel will be successful and that you anticipate using in a game.

Pass routes are usually broken down by the distance that the receiver runs off the line before executing his pass pattern. The three general areas are *short* (up to 5 yards), *medium* (around 10 yards), and *deep* (over 10 yards down the field). If your field is not lined, you can set up your markers (cones, flags, shirts) at the depth of the pattern to give the receivers a point of reference for making their break.

Each pass route must be coordinated with the drop of the quarterback so that the ball is delivered on time to the receiver. It is vital that your receivers run each route at the proper depth and be in position to make the catch when the quarterback is ready to deliver the ball.

On short pass routes, the quarterback will only take three steps before he delivers the ball. On medium and deep routes, the quarterback will drop back five steps.

The three basic short routes are the (1) *quick out*, (2) *hitch*, and (3) *slant*.

🏈 SHORT ROUTES

Number of players: All WRs
Equipment: Shorts or full pads, markers
Time: 2 minutes/once a week

1. The receivers form two lines.

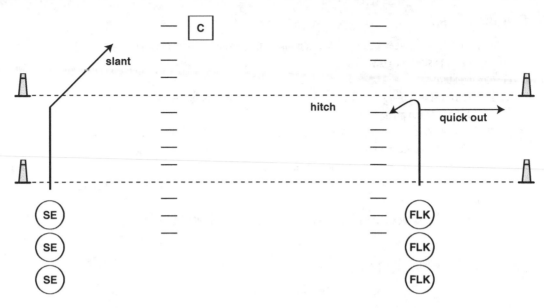

2. The first player in each line gets into his 2-point stance and listens for the coach to call out the pass route (quick out, hitch, or slant).
3. On the command of "Hut," both receivers run the pattern called (see below).
4. The players running the pattern go to the back of the line, and the next two receivers step up and get into their stances.

Coaching Points

- In the beginning of the season, the players may need to go one at a time.
- Make certain the players start correctly and drive up the field 4 yards before starting to run their pass route (see Start drill).
- Quick out route—The receiver drives 4 yards, pivots on his outside foot, and breaks to the sideline.
- Hitch route—The receiver gathers himself at 4 yards, stops his movement up the field with his outside foot, and turns back to the inside.
- Slant route—As the receiver reaches 4 yards, he angles into the center of the field.
- On all three patterns, be sure the receiver brings his head around quickly so he is looking back to the QB and has his hands up ready to make the catch.
- If your QB has trouble throwing to the outside, eliminate the quick out route completely or have your receiver move closer to the ball in his initial alignment for the quick out.

When your receivers can run the three short routes correctly, adjust the drill to teach the three medium pass patterns: (1) *out*, (2) *hook*, and (3) *in*. Each of these three pass routes are run in the 10-yard area. The actual depth is determined by the length of time your quarterback has to throw and the strength of his arm.

MEDIUM ROUTES

Number of players: All WRs
Equipment: Shorts or full pads, markers
Time: 2 minutes/once a week

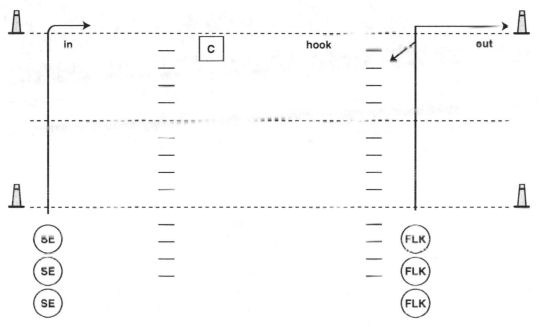

1. The wide receivers form two lines.
2. The first player in each line gets into his 2-point stance and listens for the coach to call out the pass route (out, hook, or in).
3. On the command of "Hut," both receivers run the pattern (see below).
4. The players running the pattern then go to the back of the line, and the next two receivers step up and get into their stance.

Coaching Points

- In the beginning of the season, the players may need to go one at a time.
- Make certain players start correctly and drive up the field 8 yards before running their pass route.
- Out route—The receiver drives 8 yards, pivots on his outside foot, and breaks to the sideline at 10 yards.
- Hook route—The receiver gathers himself at 9 yards, stops his movement up the field with his outside foot, and turns back to the inside at 10 yards.
- In route—The receiver drives 8 yards, pivots on his inside foot, and heads across the field to the center at 10 yards.
- On all three patterns, make certain the receiver brings his head around quickly as he makes his break so he is looking back to the QB, and that he has his hands up ready to make the catch.

The quarterback and wide receiver practice a medium route.

If your quarterback has trouble throwing to the outside you could eliminate the out route completely or have your receiver move closer to the ball in his initial alignment.

Each of these pass patterns is run in the 10 yards area and takes longer to complete. On these three patterns, the quarterback takes five steps away from the center before he sets up to throw.

In the deep area, there are two basic patterns: *post* and *up*. Again, if your quarterback lacks the arm strength to throw the ball deep, consider eliminating these two patterns.

🏈 DEEP ROUTES

Number of players: All WRs
Equipment: Shorts or full pads, markers
Time: 2 minutes/once a week

1. The wide receivers form two lines.
2. The first player in each line gets in his 2-point stance and listens for the coach to call out the pass route (up or post).
3. On the command of "Hut," both receivers run the called pattern (see below).
4. The players running the pattern go to the back of the line, and the next two receivers step up and get into their stances.

Coaching Points

• In the beginning of the season, the players may need to go one at a time.

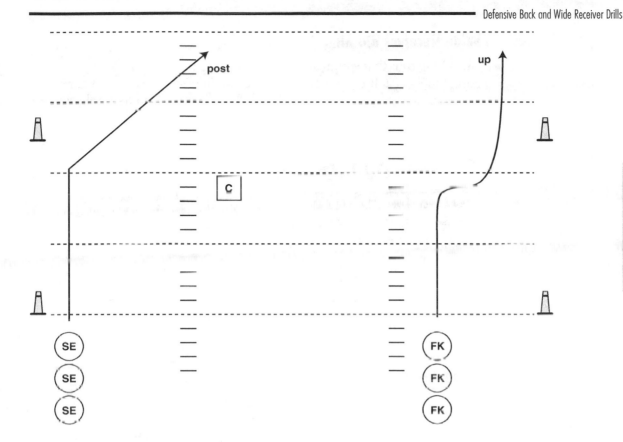

WE Deep Routes

- Make certain the players start correctly and drive up the field 10 yards before running their pass route.
- Up route—The receiver drives 10 yards, bends slightly to the outside of the defensive man, and runs straight up the field.
- Post route—The receiver drives 10 yards, then angles to the center of the field.
- On both patterns, make certain the receiver brings his head around quickly as he makes his break so he is looking back to the QB.
- Unlike the medium and short patterns, in running a deep pattern, the receiver may run 8 or 9 yards after starting his route before making the catch. It is important that he keep running as he makes the catch.
- On both deep patterns, the receiver must be ready to adjust his route—if the ball is thrown over his outside shoulder or is underthrown—by turning his head to the outside or coming back to the ball.

If your quarterback has trouble throwing deep, you may want to focus your passing attack on the short and medium passes or shorten the pattern by breaking the pass routes at 7 or 8 yards rather than 10 yards.

Each of these pass patterns takes longer to complete. On these two patterns the quarterback takes five steps away from the center before he sets up to throw as the receiver is making his break.

Wide Receiver Blocking

Most long runs that your team will have during the year will be the result of good blocking at the point of attack, then additional blocking by your wide receivers downfield on the defensive backs. It is important to emphasize to your wide receivers the importance of blocking on the run.

🏈 MIRROR BLOCKING

Number of players: All WRs
Equipment: Shorts or full pads, markers
Time: 4 minutes/once a week

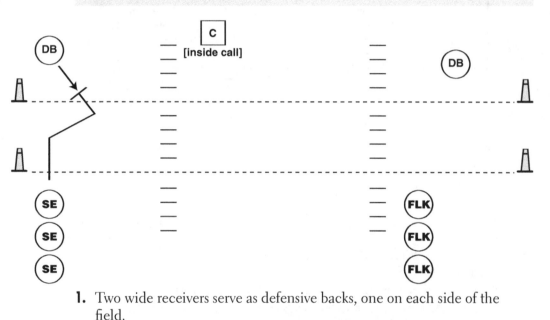

1. Two wide receivers serve as defensive backs, one on each side of the field.
2. The remaining receivers form two lines.
3. The first player in each line steps up and gets into a 2-point stance.
4. The coach calls out "inside," "off tackle," or "wide" to indicate where the ball will be run.
5. On the command of "Hut," both receivers drive off the line and get into position to block the defensive man's path to the area under attack.
6. After the player has blocked, he becomes the DB, and the player who was the DB goes to the end of his respective line.

Coaching Points

- Mirror Blocking:
  1. The receiver drives straight off the line for 4 yards and angles to the inside to a position between the DB and the ball.

2. When the receiver reaches 7 yards, he shortens his stride and turns back to the outside and facing the DB.

3. As the receiver nears the DB, he widens his feet, bends at the knees, and brings both hands up to the center of his chest in front of his numbers.

4. The receiver then mirrors the movement of the DB as he tries to get around him by shuffling his feet and staying even with the chest of the DB.

5. As they come together, the receiver punches out with the palms of both hands into the chest of the DB, then brings his hands back and sets up again, ready for the next contact.

- Try to coach your players to keep their hips over their feet and avoid lunging out at the defensive man.
- In the beginning of the season, players may need to go one at a time.

WR Mirror Blocking

Defensive and Offensive Line and Tight End Drills

Defensive Line Drills

Offensive linemen have the advantage of knowing both where the ball is going to be run (or thrown) and when the play will begin. Because of these factors, the drills for your defensive line must be reactionary, and the players prepared to adjust on the move to each particular play.

The more your defensive linemen learn to recognize who is blocking them, what blocks they are using, and how to react to defeat the block, the better they will play.

Start the following drills for the defensive line by moving the ball and not by a vocal command. This makes your defensive linemen focus on the ball and move on the snap.

4-POINT STANCE

Number of players: All DLs
Equipment: Shorts or full pads, markers
Time: 2 minutes/every day

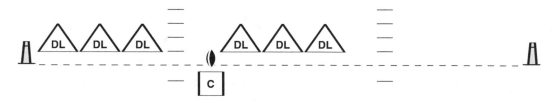

1. All the DLs line up across the field facing the coach.
2. On the command of "Set," each player bends his knees and rests his forearms on the inside of each thigh (see below).

3. On the command of "Stance," each player assumes a 4-point stance (see below).
4. The coach scans down the line making certain that everyone is properly set.
5. On the command of "Up," the players come out of their stance to an upright position.

Coaching Points

- Have players line up with their feet even, spread shoulder width, in an upright stance.
- For the "Set" position, players bend their knees, keep their backs straight, heads up, and rest their forearms on the inside of each thigh.
- 4-Point Stance:
  1. On the command of "Stance," each player reaches out with both arms and places both hands on the ground in front of his shoulders.
  2. His weight is resting on the balls of both feet, and his hips are up, even with or higher than his shoulder pads. Check that your players do not have their hands too far forward, and they are not lowering their hips to be more comfortable.
  3. His back is straight, with his shoulders even, head up, and eyes looking at the ball.
- In the beginning of the year, go one player at a time until you are confident that each player understands how to start correctly

Defensive lineman in a 4-point stance.

Adjusting to a 3-Point Stance

You may want to have your defensive linemen, especially your defensive ends (the players lined up in front of the offensive tackle or to the outside), use a 3-point stance with only one hand on the ground.

This is easily achieved by having them assume a correct 4-point stance, then lift one hand off the ground. Have them place the arm that's not on the ground such that the forearm is resting on the inside of the thigh, palm up, and facing straight ahead with the fingers open.

Often when first learning the 3-point stance, a player will put his hand on the ground (the *down hand*) more toward the center of his body, and not straight down from his shoulder. You will be able to see this when you observe him in his stance—his shoulders will not be even and his body will be cocked to one side.

Using a balanced 3-point stance may make it easier for your players to rush the passer. A player will also be able to stagger his feet by stepping back with the foot on the side of his "down hand" (the hand on the ground). The more weight a player has on his down hand and forward foot, the quicker he can charge across the line to rush the passer.

Defensive lineman in a 3-point stance.

On most defenses, it is better to have your defensive linemen—who line up in front of an offensive guard or center—stay in a 4-point stance to keep them balanced in their stance.

🏈 START

Number of players: All DLs
Equipment: Shorts or full pads, markers
Time: 2 minutes/every day

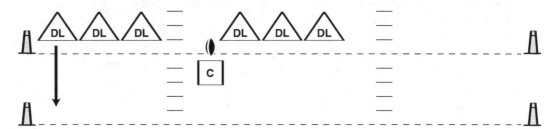

1. All DLs line up across the field facing the coach.
2. On the coach's command of "Set," each player bends his knees and rests his forearms on the inside of each thigh.
3. On the command of "Stance," each player assumes a 4-point stance and looks at the ball.
4. Once the players are properly in their stance, the coach grasps the ball and simulates a snap (by pulling the ball toward him), having the players charge straight ahead for three or four steps (see below).
5. The players return to their original positions and repeat the drill.

Coaching Points

- In the beginning of the year, go one player at a time until you are confident that each player is looking at the ball and starts as soon as the ball moves.
- Charging the Ball:
  1. The players move on the ball, charging straight ahead, using short steps, and keeping their feet wide as they charge.
  2. As they charge, their shoulders are low. You should not be able to see the front of their chest.
  3. Both hands come up, with palms forward and fingers open, as they start their charge.
  4. The players have their heads up and eyes open, with their arms moving in a normal running action, as they continue across the line.

Shedding Run Blocks

When teaching your defensive linemen the individual blocks they will face (and have to defeat), have them work as partners, with each player reacting to the block and then moving over to play as the offensive blocker.

In the beginning, have the defensive lineman and the blocker go at half speed. Everyone should understand that these are drills designed to teach defensive players to react to a variety of blocks and are not drills designed to create maximum contact.

As a coach it is important for you to decide the blocks your defensive linemen will face. In the beginning of the year, this will be based on your team's offense, then later in the year on your opponent's attack. Individual time should be spent on learning to defeat these blocks.

As you design your defense, you will be able to tell each defensive lineman which gap is his primary responsibility. When reacting to the various blocks, he should be coached to keep his head on the side of his gap responsibility.

Go one player at a time when you are first teaching block protection to your defensive linemen.

Teaching the Order of Who Will Block the Player and How

Before teaching players the techniques for defeating the variety of blocks they will face, it is important to give them an understanding of who can block them and the type of block each offensive player can use. This is called *block progression*, and hopefully it will be the way your defensive players learn to anticipate and recognize what is happening as the ball is snapped.

Each defensive player, and especially the defensive linemen, must understand the natural progression to follow on every defensive play. This progression consists of the following:

1. Moving forward on the center snap.
2. Seeing who is trying to block him.
3. Recognizing the type of block being used.
4. Reacting to the block.
5. Shedding the block.
6. Locating and moving to the ball carrier.

🏈 LEARNING BLOCKERS

Number of players: All DLs
Equipment: Shorts or full pads
Time: 2 minutes/once a week

1. This is a mental drill and does not require movement.
2. Players form two lines facing the coach. The players simulating the offensive players are on one knee.
3. The defensive players stand up so they can point out the order in which the blockers can attack them.

```
/DE\   /DT\  —  /NT\   /DT\   /DE\        —
                     —                         —
              - - - - -  (●) - - - - - - - - - - - - - - - - - - -
 (TE)  (OT)  (OG)  — [C]   (OG)  (OT)  (TE)—
```

4. The coach points to each player on defense and has him point and call out the order of the blockers and say the type of block each will use.

5. The players then go from offense to defense until every defensive lineman has gone through the drill.

Coaching Points

- For the DEs, the read is OT first with a drive or hook block; TE second with a down block; OG third with a hook block.
- For the DTs, the read is OG first with a drive or hook block; OT second with a down block, CN third with a hook block.
- For the NT, the read is CN first with a drive or hook block; OG to the side of the play second with a down block or OG opposite the side of the play third with a hook block.
- Emphasize to your defensive linemen that this should be their thinking prior to the start of each play.

Defeating the Run Blocks from the Player in Front of You

🏈 DRIVE BLOCK PROTECTION

Number of players: All DLs
Equipment: Full pads
Time: 4 minutes/twice a week

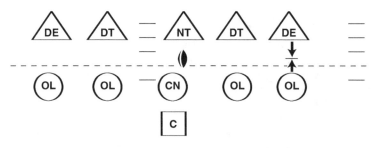

1. All the defensive linemen line up across the field facing the coach.

2. The coach tells the defensive players their gap responsibility, either right or left.

3. On command, each player on offense and defense gets into his stance.

4. The defensive players focus on the ball.

5. On the command of "Hut," the CN makes the snap, and the blockers move forward to drive block the defensive player in front of them.
6. The defensive player reacts to the block.
7. The coach calls out "Stop" or blows a whistle to stop the drill
8. The offensive and defensive players change positions and repeat the drill.

Coaching Points

- Drive Block Protection:
  1. When the ball is snapped, the defensive player charges forward using short, powerful steps.
  2. As he comes forward, he keeps his shoulder pads under the pads of the offensive blocker.
  3. He brings both arms forward, hitting the blocker in the chest with the palms of both hands.
  4. As he makes contact, he slides his head to the side of his gap responsibility and extends his arms, separating from the blocker.
  5. He then attempts to drive the blocker back across the line of scrimmage.

🏈 HOOK BLOCK PROTECTION

Number of players: All DLs
Equipment: Full pads
Time: 4 minutes/twice a week

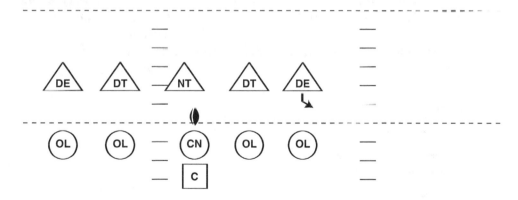

1. All the defensive linemen line up across the field facing the coach.
2. The DEs and DTs line up on the outside shoulder of the blockers, and the NT lines up on the left or right of the CN.
3. On command, each player on offense and defense gets into his stance on the appropriate shoulder of the defensive man.
4. The defensive players focus on the ball.
5. On the command of "Hut," the CN makes the snap, and the blockers step to the side designated by the coach to hook block the defensive player in front of them.

6. The defensive player reacts to the block (see below).

7. The coach calls out "Stop" or blows a whistle to stop the drill.

8. The offensive and defensive players swap positions and repeat the drill.

Coaching Points

- Hook Block Protection:
  1. As the defensive lineman starts his charge on the snap, he should see the head and upper body of the blocker moving to his outside.
  2. When he sees this action, he fires both hands straight ahead to make contact with the shoulder pad and upper body of the blocker.
  3. He then continues to extend his arms.
  4. At this point, he separates from the blocker and drives the blocker down the line of scrimmage toward the ball.
- When performing this block protection, it is important for the defensive man to keep his head on the same side of the blocker as his gap responsibility.

Shedding a Passing Block from the Side

In the two previous blocks, the defensive player was reacting to the block of an offensive player lined up in front of him. This type of block (*drive* or *hook*), with the offensive player in front of him, is what your defensive linemen will face the majority of the time.

The next block that your defensive lineman will have to recognize and learn to defeat is a block coming from his right or left from a second offensive blocker. This is a *down block* or *angle block* and usually comes from a blocker on the outside of the defensive lineman (although it also may come from a blocker lined up closer to the ball).

🏈 DOWN BLOCK PROTECTION

Number of players: All DLs
Equipment: Full pads
Time: 4 minutes/twice a week

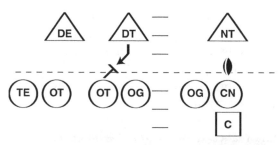

1. The defensive linemen line up in three groups of three players with space between each group.

2. The DL lines up directly in front of the appropriate blocker (DE↔OT, DT↔OG, N ↔CN).
3. On command, the players get into their stances.
4. The defensive player focuses on the ball.
5. On the command of "Hut," the CN makes the snap.
6. The blocker directly in front of the defensive player moves away laterally (to his right) from his offensive partner.
7. The other blocker attempts to down block on the defensive player.
8. The defensive player reacts to the block.
9. The coach calls out "Stop" or blows a whistle to stop the drill.
10. The offensive blocker and defensive player change positions.
11. Repeat the drill until all three players have had their turns.

Coaching Points

- Set up the drill the next day with the defensive players on the other side.
- If you are not using an NT on your defensive front, eliminate this group from the drill.
- Down Block Protection:
    1. On the ball snap, the defensive player moves straight ahead.
    2. When he sees that the man in front of him is not going to block him, he steps toward the blocker coming from his side.
    3. As he takes this short step, he must stay low.
    4. He meets the blocker with his shoulder pad and forearm on the side of the block—i.e., if the blocker is approaching from his right, he meets the blocker with his right shoulder pad and forearm.
    5. He then brings the palm of his other hand around and makes contact with the shoulder pads of the blocker.
- Emphasize to the defensive player that he needs to hold his position.
- If the defensive player is able to get separation from the blocker, he should move to the outside on the defensive side of the line of scrimmage.

Reacting to Three Potential Blockers

As the year progresses and you feel that your defensive linemen are reacting properly to the drive, hook, and down bocks, you can create a drill where the defensive player has to look and react to all three blocks.

🏈 3-BLOCK PROTECTION

Number of players: All DLs
Equipment: Full pads, ball
Time: 4 minutes/once a week (later in the year)

1. The coach huddles up the three offensive players and designates which player is the blocker and what type of block he will use.

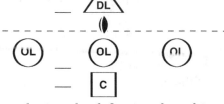

2. The coach gives the defensive player his gap responsibility and the offensive players the snap count (1 or 2 hut) and brings them up to the line.
3. The ball is then snapped on the coach's command, and the block is executed.
4. The defensive player sees and reacts properly to defeat the offensive blocker.
5. The coach calls out "Stop" or blows a whistle to stop the drill.
6. The position of the ball can be moved to the right or left in relationship to the player's actual position.

Coaching Points

- This is a more advanced drill for your defensive linemen and should only be used when you feel that they can recognize and defeat each block individually.
- Make certain that the defensive player is reading the block and reacting appropriately.

Rushing the Passer

The next individual block that your defensive linemen need to react to is a *pass protection block*. This block is different in that the blocker is retreating off the line of scrimmage and not firing out on the snap of the ball. The challenge for the defensive player is to quickly recognize that it is a pass and to immediately attack toward the quarterback.

Prior to the start of the drill, mark the field exactly where the quarterback will be setting up to throw. This marking gives your defensive linemen a target area to reach. You can adjust the position of the defensive rush man from head-to-head to the outside shoulder of the blocker to give each blocker a different picture of the rush.

Because you have rush men charging the quarterback and blockers moving back off the line, it is best to only have one defensive rusher and one blocker go at a time.

TARGET RUSH

Number of players: All DLs
Equipment: Shorts or full pads, markers, ball
Time: 2 minutes/twice a week

1. Place a marker, or a stand-up blocking dummy if one is available, directly behind the ball, 7 yards off the line of scrimmage.

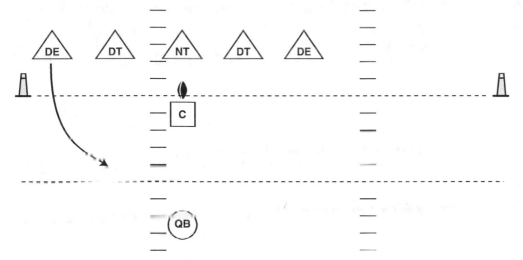

2. Alert each defensive lineman that the marker represents the QB and it is the point they are sprinting to reach.

3. On the command of "Stance," the designated player assumes his stance and looks at the ball.

4. Once the player is properly set, the coach grasps the ball, simulates a snap (by pulling the ball toward him), and has the players charge up the field toward the QB with three or four short steps, then sprint.

5. The players return to their original positions and repeat the drill.

Coaching Points

- Make certain the players are stepping forward on the snap.
- Target Rush:
  1. The initial charge is low but rises as the defensive linemen move toward the QB target area.
  2. As they start their charge, both hands come up with palms forward and fingers open.
  3. The players' heads are up and eyes open with their arms moving in a normal running action as they continue across the line.
  4. Emphasize that they need to run past the QB target area—not stop when they reach it.

Basic Pass Rush Techniques

Once your defensive linemen are charging across the line and taking a proper path to the quarterback area, you can teach them basic pass rush techniques: the *bull pass rush* and the *jerk pass rush*. As you begin instruction in this area, explain to your defensive linemen that there are numerous ways they can influence the opponent's passing attack:

- They can force the passer to throw before he is ready.
- They can reach up and deflect a pass, changing the path of the ball.
- They can tackle the quarterback before he has a chance to pass.
- They can make an interception on a ball batted up in the air.

Any one of these actions will greatly help your pass defense.

Your defensive lineman is reacting to the block against him when he is playing defensive line on running plays. The offense knows where the ball is going to be run. The initial advantage is slanted to the offense.

This changes when an offensive lineman sets back to pass protect. Now the defensive man is the one who decides where and how he will rush the quarterback. The offensive man must react to his charge and movements. If the defensive lineman knows ahead of the snap how and where he is going to rush, the advantage shifts to the defensive player.

🏈 BULL PASS RUSH

Number of players: All DLs
Equipment: Shorts or full pads, ball
Time: 3 minutes/twice a week

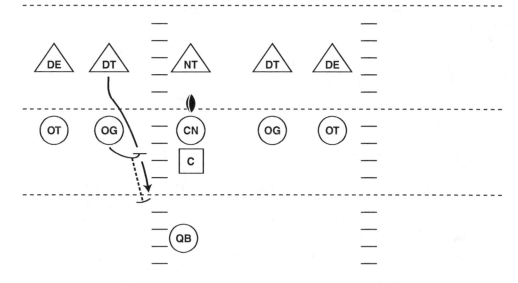

1. The coach designates a defensive rush man and blocker to execute the drill.
2. Prior to starting the drill, the rush man locates the spot where the QB will be set up.
3. The defensive rusher pictures rushing through the blocker to the QB spot.
4. The CN snaps the ball on the command of "Hut," and the blocker sets up to pass protect.
5. The defensive player must see the ball snapped and the blocker setting up before he begins his pass rush.
6. The coach calls out "Stop" or blows a whistle to stop the drill.

7. The rush man changes position with the player on offense.
8. The coach has the next two players perform the drill.

Coaching Points

- When first teaching the pass rush technique, have the defensive player rush at half speed.
- Make certain the rusher is stepping forward on the snap.
- Bull Pass Rush:
  1. The rusher's initial charge is low but rises as he moves toward the blocker.
  2. As he starts his charge, both hands come up, with the palms forward and fingers open.
  3. The rusher has his head up and eyes open, with his arms moving in a normal running action, as he continues across the line.
  4. When the rusher is close enough to the blocker, he drives the palms of both hands under the blocker's shoulder pads.
  5. As his hands make contact with the armpit area of the blocker, he extends his arms, creating separation, and pushes up and back as he continues to drive his legs in short choppy steps.
- Emphasize to the rusher that his goal is to push the blocker straight back into the QB target.

The bull pass rush is one of the easiest pass rush techniques to learn and is aided by the natural backward movement of the offensive blocker. Teach the pass rusher to anticipate and expect the blocker to take a stand (stop his backward movement and lunge forward) once the offensive blocker has been pushed back into the quarterback. When this happens, the defensive rusher must be ready to use the jerk pass rush technique to get by the blocker and move to the quarterback target area.

 **JERK PASS RUSH**

Number of players: All DLs
Equipment: Shorts or full pads
Time: 3 minutes/twice a week

1. The coach chooses a defensive rush man and blocker to perform the drill.
2. Prior to starting the drill, the rush man locates the spot where the QB will be set up.
3. The coach designates on which side of the blocker (right or left) he wants the rusher to go.
4. The defensive rusher pictures rushing around the blocker on the designated side to the QB spot.
5. The CN snaps the ball on the command of "Hut," and the blocker sets up to pass protect.
6. The defensive player must see the ball snapped and the OL setting up, then begin his pass rush.

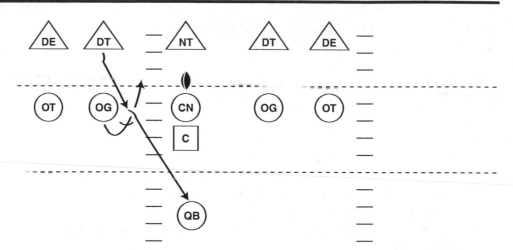

7. The offensive lineman stops his backward movement and lunges forward when the rusher nears him.

8. The coach calls out "Stop" or blows a whistle to stop the drill.

9. The rush man changes position with the player on offense.

10. The coach selects two different players to perform the drill.

Coaching Points

- When first teaching pass rush technique, have the defensive player rush at half speed.
- Make certain the rusher steps forward on the snap.
- Jerk Pass Rush:
    1. The rusher's initial charge is low but rises as he moves toward the offensive blocker.
    2. As he starts his charge, both hands come up, with the palms forward and fingers open.
    3. The rusher has his head up and eyes open, with his arms moving in a normal running action, as he continues across the line.
    4. When the rusher sees the blocker setting up and lunging forward, he reaches out with both hands and grabs the blocker's jersey.
    5. The rusher uses the forward lunge of the blocker to pull the blocker to the side opposite the way he is going to rush (rush left—pull right; rush right—pull left).
    6. The rusher steps across the blocker's body with the leg and foot on the side that he is jerking the blocker, which allows the rusher to get clear of the block.
    7. Once he is past the blocker, the rusher must sprint to the QB target area.

These two pass rush techniques are the easiest to teach and seem to be natural movements for young players. Your time will be well spent teaching and perfecting these two pass rush techniques rather than taking valuable time trying to introduce more complex rush techniques.

Offensive Line Drills/Tight End Drills

Offensive linemen have the advantage of knowing both where the ball is going to be run (or thrown) and when the play will begin. They need to use this advantage by moving as the ball is snapped before the defensive player starts his charge.

Offensive linemen need to understand where the ball is going to be run and anticipate any movement by the defensive players in that direction.

Start the following drills for the offensive line by a vocal command. This makes your offensive linemen focus on the snap count as they would in a game.

4-POINT STANCE

Number of players: All OLs and TEs
Equipment: Shorts or full pads
Time: 2 minutes/every day

```
          ___      ___
               c
                                    ___
      ___                        ___

 (OL) (OL) (OL) (OL) (OL) (OL) (OL) (TE) ― (TE)
```

1. All the OLs and TEs line up across the field facing the coach.
2. On the command of "Set," each player bends his knees and rests his forearms on the inside of each thigh.
3. On the command of "Stance," each player assumes a 4-point stance (see below).
4. The coach scans down the line checking that everyone is in a proper stance.
5. On the command of "Up," the players come out of their stances to an upright position.

Coaching Points

- 4-Point Stance:
  1. Have the players line up with their feet even, spread shoulder-width apart, in an upright stance.
  2. When they go to the "Set" position, players bend their knees, keeping their backs straight and heads up, and rest their forearms on the inside of each thigh.
  3. On the command of "Stance," each player reaches out with both arms and places both hands on the ground slightly in front of his shoulders.
  4. His hips are up, back straight, shoulders even, and head up.

Offensive lineman in a 4-point stance.

Offensive lineman in a
3-point stance.

- Check that your players do not have their hands too far forward, and they are not lowering their hips to be more comfortable.
- In the beginning of the year, go one player at a time until you are confident that each player understands how to start correctly.

If you want your offensive linemen or tight ends to use a 3-point stance with only one hand on the ground, have them assume a correct four-point stance, then lift one hand. The hand that's not on the ground can be placed so that the forearm rests on the inside of the thigh.

If you teach the 3-point stance first, often the player will put his down hand (the hand on the ground) more into the center of his body and not straight down from his shoulder. When you observe him in his stance, his shoulders will be uneven and his body will be cocked to one side.

Using a balanced 3-point stance may make it easier for players to pull laterally to the right or left and to set up to block on pass plays.

START

Number of players: All OLs/TEs
Equipment: Shorts or full pads
Time: 2 minutes/every day

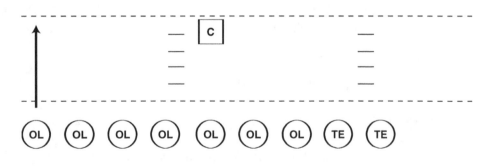

1. All the OLs/TEs line up across the field facing the coach.
2. On the command of "Set," each player bends his knees and rests his forearms on the inside of each thigh.
3. On command, each player assumes a 4-point stance.
4. The coach calls out "Hut," and the players charge straight ahead for three or four steps (see below).
5. The players return to their original positions and repeat the drill.

Coaching Points

- In the beginning of the year, go one player at a time until you are confident that each player understands how to start correctly.
- Moving on the Ball:
  1. The players move on the ball, charging straight ahead, using short steps, and keeping their feet wide as they charge.
  2. As they charge, their shoulders are low. You should not be able to see the front of their chest.
  3. Both hands come up, with palms forward and fingers open.
  4. The players have their heads up and eyes open, with their arms moving in a normal running action, as they continue across the line.

Individual Run Blocks

When teaching individual blocks to your offensive linemen and tight ends, have the players work as partners with each player executing the block and then moving over to play as the defensive lineman.

In the beginning you may have the defensive lineman hold a bag, or if a blocking bag is not available, you can have him go at half speed. These drills are designed to teach offensive blocking and not to create maximum contact.

As a coach, it is important for you to decide which blocks your offensive linemen and tight ends will have to learn and perfect. Time should be spent only on the blocks that your players need. In the beginning of the year, work only on the blocks your offensive line and tight ends will be called upon to use in games.

The blocking drills can include the tight ends if there is not a tight end coach on your staff. The coach or another center should always take the snap from the center whenever the center is involved in making a block.

🏈 DRIVE BLOCK

Number of players: All OLs/TEs
Equipment: Shorts or full pads, markers, and blocking bag (optional)
Time: 4 minutes/twice a week

1. The DLs line up directly in front of the offensive linemen.
2. The coach calls out which shoulder the blocker BK will use in his drive block (right or left).
3. The coach calls out "Down," and the players get into their stances.
4. On the command of "Hut," each blocker drives into his designated DL and makes contact with the shoulder indicated by the coach.
5. Each blocker drives his man back for 2 or 3 yards.
6. The blocker and DL exchange positions.

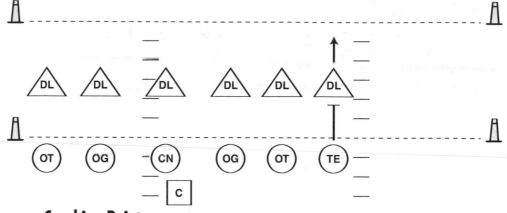

Coaching Points

- In the beginning of the year, go one player at a time until you are confident that each player understands how to start correctly.
- Drive Block:
  1. The offensive lineman comes off low as in the Start drill and gets under the shoulder pads of the DL.
  2. The offensive lineman takes short powerful steps and explodes off the foot on the side of his shoulder block as contact is made.
  3. As he makes contact with the designated shoulder, he slides his head to the hip of the DL and drives the palm on the side of his shoulder block into the chest of the DL.
  4. Once he makes contact, offensive lineman keeps driving with short steps, driving back and up while attempting to move the DL back off the line of scrimmage.

Second Blocks

In the *hook block*, the offensive lineman or tight end will be blocking a defensive lineman who is lined up on his outside shoulder. This block will require the blocker to move laterally and not straight ahead on his first step. His goal will be to stop any penetration by the defensive player across the line and then block him back off the line of scrimmage.

🏈 HOOK BLOCK

Number of players: All OLs/TEs
Equipment: Shorts or full pads, markers, and blocking dummy (optional)
Time: 4 minutes/twice a week

1. The DL lines up on the outside shoulders of the OT and TE in preparation to charge straight ahead.
2. When the coach calls "Down," the players get into their stances.
3. On the command of "Hut," each blocker steps laterally to stop their DL from crossing the line. Each blocker drives his man back for 2 or 3 yards.

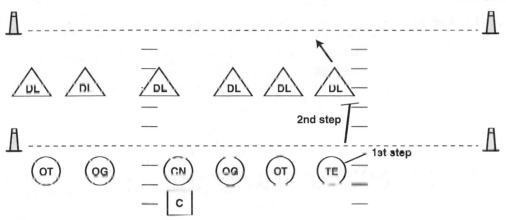

4. The blockers and DLs exchange positions.

Coaching Points

- In the beginning of the season, drill one player at a time until you're confident that each can execute the block properly.
- Hook Block:
  1. The first step the blocker makes is low and lateral to the foot on the side of the defensive player.
  2. With this step, the blocker's body turns to the outside, allowing his head to be in front of the DL.
  3. The second step, with his other foot, is straight at the center of the DL's body.
  4. As he makes this step, he drives the palm of his hand (on the side of the second step) directly into the chest of the DL to stop his charge.
  5. As his head slips to the outside of the DL, he takes his other hand and drives it under the DL's outside shoulder pad.
  6. From this position, the blocker drives the DL back and to the inside for 2 or 3 yards.

Third Block

In the next block, the *down block*, the offensive lineman or tight end blocks a defensive lineman who is lined up in front of an adjacent offensive player, usually to his inside. This block requires the blocker to move laterally and not straight ahead on his first step. His goal is to stop any penetration by the defensive player across the line, then block him down the line of scrimmage and away from the path of the ball carrier.

 DOWN BLOCK

Number of players: All OLs/TEs
Equipment: Shorts or full pads, markers, and blocking dummy (optional)
Time: 4 minutes/twice a week

1. The defensive linemen line up directly in front of the offensive linemen

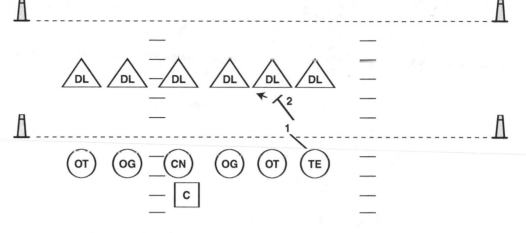

and charge straight ahead. If using a blocking dummy, the DL should turn the dummy so it faces the offensive blocker.

2. When blocking as a group, only the CN and one side of blockers go at a time. The coach designates who is blocking prior to each snap.

3. The coach calls "Down," and the players get into their stances.

4. On the command of "Hut," each blocker steps laterally to stop the DLs from crossing the line. Each blocker drives his man down the line for 1 or 2 yards.

5. The blocker and DL exchange positions.

Coaching Points

- In the beginning of the season, drill one player at a time until you are confident that each can execute the block properly.
- Down Block:
  1. The first blocker step is at an angle toward the DL with his foot nearest the man he is blocking.
  2. The blocker should anticipate the DL moving forward and not step to where he originally lined up.
  3. With this step, the blocker turns his body and stays low as he blocks into the side of the DL.
  4. The blocker's second step, with the foot away from the DL, is his explosion foot. He drives his shoulder pad on the side of the second step into the side of the DL.
  5. As he makes contact with the DL's shoulder pad, the blocker drives the palm of the hand on that side into the hip area of the DL.
  6. The blocker then drives the DL down the line of scrimmage.

Blocking on Pass Plays

The next individual block to teach is a *pass protection block*. This block is different because the blocker retreats *off* the line of scrimmage instead of firing out on the ball snap. The challenge for the blocker is to get set up and move into position between the defensive rush man and the quarterback.

It is good to have the tight end work on this block because there may be game situations where you need to protect your quarterback, giving him extra time to pass. Keeping the tight end in to pass protect may be the best solution.

Prior to the start of the drill, mark on the field exactly where the quarterback will set up to throw. This marking gives your pass protection blockers a point of reference for their body position.

You can adjust the position of the defensive rush man from head up to outside shoulder to give each blocker a different picture of the rush.

Because you have blockers moving backwards and rush men charging to the quarterback, it is safest to have only one blocker and one defensive rusher go at a time.

PASS PROTECTION BLOCK

Number of players: All OLs/TEs
Equipment: Shorts or full pads
Time: 5 minutes/twice a week

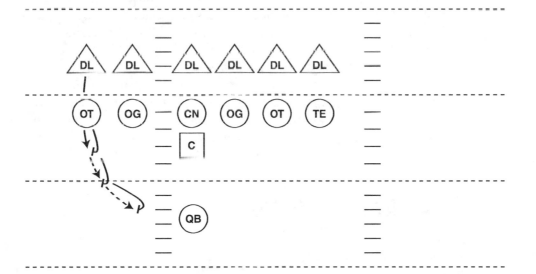

1. Designate a blocker and rush man.
2. Prior to starting the drill, have each blocker turn back to see the spot where the QB will be.
3. When the coach calls out "Down," the blocker gets into his stance.
4. On the command of "Hut," the blocker moves off the line as the designated rusher starts his rush and attempts to reach the QB spot.
5. The blocker stays in front of the rusher until the coach calls out "Stop."
6. The blocker switches to the defensive position once he has executed the block correctly.

Coaching Points

- When teaching pass protection blocking, have the defensive player rush at half speed.
- Pass Protection Block:
  1. On the command of "Hut," the blocker pushes off his hands and steps back off the line.
  2. If the rusher is directly in front of the blocker, the blocker's first step back is with his inside foot to protect the fast line to the QB. If the rusher is lined up to the outside, the blocker's first step back is with his outside foot, putting him in a position to stop an outside rush.
  3. As the blocker retreats off the line, he takes short shuffling steps, bringing his hands up to the center of his chest, with the palms facing forward.
  4. When the rusher starts to get close, the blocker chops his steps, bends his knees, and prepares to make contact, keeping his back straight and head up.
  5. On contact, the blocker explodes into the rusher by extending both arms and driving his palms into the rusher's chest.
  6. Once the rusher is stopped, the blocker brings his hands back and sets up again to repeat the maneuver.

Learning the Basic Pass Routes

I've included the tight ends with the offensive linemen in this chapter because on most youth teams the tight end *blocks first* on all running plays and *then* becomes a receiver on the passing attack. In addition to blocking, the tight end needs to learn to run pass routes correctly and catch the ball.

The following tight end drills stress the basic pass routes (or pass patterns) used in a passing attack. The patterns you feature will depend on the passing ability of your quarterback, the ability of your offensive line to pass protect, and the catching ability of your wide receivers. Spend a majority of your time in practice throwing the passes that you anticipate using in a game.

The two basic short routes are *short* and *looking*.

SHORT PASS ROUTES

Number of players: All TEs
Equipment: Shorts or full pads, markers
Time: 2 minutes/once a week

1. Each TE lines up in his 3-point stance and listens for the coach to call out the pass route (short or looking).
2. Another TE lines up as a linebacker directly in front of the TE running the pass route.
3. On the command of "Hut," both receivers run the pattern called (see below).
4. After running the pattern, the TEs go to the LB position, the LBs go to the back of the line, and the next two TEs step up and get into their stance.

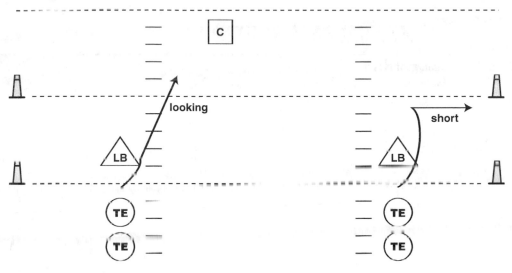

Coaching Points

- In the beginning of the season, the players may need to go one at a time.
- Make certain the players release on the correct side of the LB and drive up the field 4 yards before starting to run their pass route.
- Short pattern— The TE releases outside of the LB, drives 4 yards, then pivots on his outside foot, breaking to the sideline.
- Looking pattern—The TE releases inside of the LB and angles in to the center of the field.
- On both short patterns, make certain the TE brings his head around quickly so he is looking back to the QB for the ball, and that his hands are up, ready to make the catch.

Patterns up the Field

When your receivers can run the two short routes correctly, adjust the drill to teach the three medium pass patterns: *out, center,* and *cross.* These three patterns take more time and are run at a distance farther from the line of scrimmage. It is best to have one tight end run the out route while the other runs the cross pattern to avoid collision. Both players can run the center route at the same time.

Tight end in a 3-point stance.

MEDIUM PASS ROUTES

Number of players: All TEs
Equipment: Shorts or full pads, markers
Time: 2 minutes/once a week

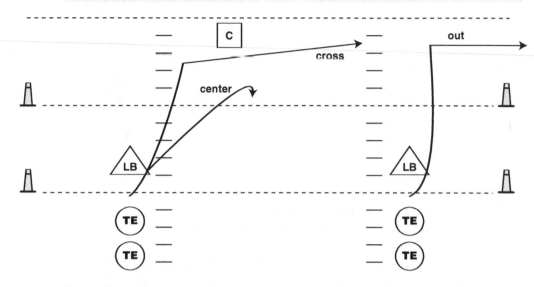

1. Each TE lines up in his 3-point stance and listens for the coach to call out the pass route (out, center, or cross).
2. Another TE lines up as a linebacker directly in front of the TE running the pass route.
3. On the command of "Hut," both receivers run the pattern that's been called (see below).
4. The players running the pattern go to the LB position, and the LB goes to the back of the line.
5. The next two TEs step up and get into their stance.

Coaching Points

- In the beginning of the season, the players may need to go one at a time.
- Make certain that the players release on the correct side of the LB and drive 8 yards up the field before running their pass routes.
- Out pattern—The TE releases outside of the LB, drives 8 yards, then pivots on his outside foot, breaking to the sideline.
- Center route—The TE releases inside of the LB and angles in to the center of the field. At 8 yards he stops and turns back to the line of scrimmage.
- Cross pattern—The TE releases inside of the LB and angles in to the center of the field. At 8 yards he pivots on his inside foot, then continues running across the field.
- On all three patterns, make certain the TE brings his head around quickly so he is looking back to the QB for the ball, and that he has his hands up, ready to make the catch.

Going Deep

During a game, it is the pass coverage and the defensive style of your opponent that determines when you can throw deep to your tight end. You may find that the defense always has a defensive back deep in the center of the field, and it will be impossible to throw into this area of the field.

As the game progresses, try to determine if there is an opportunity for your tight end to get deep downfield. Also take into consideration the speed of your tight end, your quarterback's arm strength, and the ability of your offensive line to pass protect. All three areas need to function well in order to complete a deep pass pattern, especially to your tight end.

The two deep routes are *up* (or *post*) and *seam*.

🏈 DEEP PASS ROUTES

Number of players: All TEs
Equipment: Shorts or full pads, markers
Time: 2 minutes/once a week

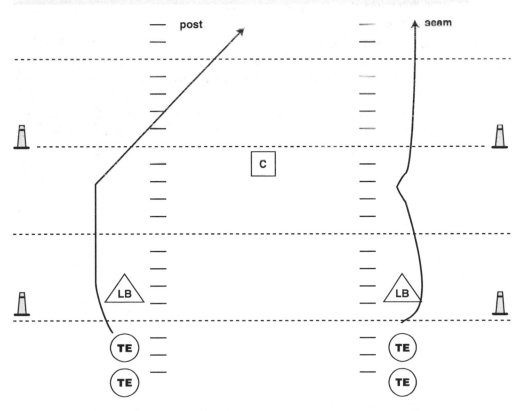

1. The first TE in each line lines up in his 3-point stance and listens for the coach to call out the pass route (post or seam).

2. Another TE lines up as a linebacker directly in front of the TE running the pass route.

3. On the command of "Hut," both receivers run the pattern that's been called (see below).

4. The players who ran the pattern then go to the back of the line, and the next two receivers step up and get into their stance.

Coaching Points

- In the beginning of the season, the players may need to go one at a time.
- Make certain the players release on the correct side of the LB and drive 8 yards up the field before running their pass route.
- Seam pattern—The TE releases outside of the LB, drives 8 yards, bends to the outside for 2 yards, and runs straight up the field just outside of the hash marks.
- Post pattern—The TE releases outside of the LB and runs straight up the field for 8 yards, angling in toward the center as he runs deep.
- On both of these patterns, make certain the TE brings his head around quickly as he makes his break so he is looking back to the QB for the ball.
- Unlike the medium and short patterns, deep patterns call for the TE to run an additional 8 or 9 yards after starting his pattern before making the catch. It's important that he keeps running to catch the ball.
- On both patterns, the TE must adjust his route—in case the ball is thrown over his outside shoulder or is underthrown—by turning his head to the outside or coming back for the ball.
- If your QB has trouble throwing deep, focus your passing attack on the short and medium passes, or shorten the pattern by breaking the pass routes at 6 yards rather than 8.
- Each of these pass patterns takes longer to complete. On these two patterns, the QB takes five steps away from the center before he sets up to throw as the TE is making his break.

Linebacker
and Running Back Drills

Linebacker Drills

Offensive linemen have the advantage of knowing where the ball is going to be run (or thrown) and when the play will begin. Linebackers, on the other hand, need to be reactionary, and must be taught to adjust, on the move, to what is happening on each particular play.

The more your linebackers learn to recognize who is blocking them, which block they are using, and how they need to react to defeat the block, the better your defense will be.

All the following linebacker drills are started by moving the ball and not by a vocal command. This teaches your linebackers to stay in position, watch the ball, and move on the snap.

2-POINT STANCE

Number of players: All LBs
Equipment: Shorts or full pads
Time: 2 minutes/every day

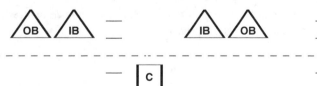

1. All linebackers line up across the field facing the coach.
2. On the coach's command of "Stance," each player bends his knees and gets in the proper stance (see below).

LB 2-Point Stance

Inside linebacker stance. (left)

Outside linebacker stance when opposite a blocker. (right)

3. The coach scans down the line making certain that everyone is properly set.
4. On the coaches command of "Up," the players rise to an upright position.

Coaching Points

- In the beginning of the year, go one player at a time until you are confident that each player understands his stance.
- 2-Point Stance:
  1. Have the players line up with their feet even, spread shoulder-width apart, in an upright stance.
  2. All players bend their knees, position their shoulders slightly in front of their hips, and keep their backs straight and heads up. OBs should adjust their feet so their outside foot is back.
  3. The IBs, and any OB who plays in front of an offensive lineman or TE, keep their elbows in at their sides and their palms up and in front of their chests, with fingers spread.
  4. An OB who plays in "space" (without a blocker directly in front of him) may narrow his stance and allow his arms to hang down in a relaxed manner.

START

Number of players: All LBs
Equipment: Shorts or full pads
Time: 2 minutes/every day

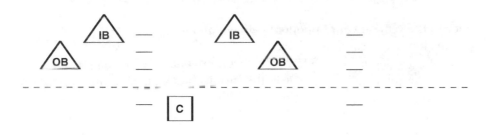

1. Four linebackers line up across the field facing the coach. (If you only use three linebackers, then have only three line up in their appropriate positions.)
2. On the command of "Stance," each player assumes his appropriate 2-point stance in a position to see the ball, with the IBs 4 yards off the ball.
3. Once the players are set properly, the coach grasps the ball and simulates a snap (by slapping or pulling the ball toward him), then he moves wide to his right or left or steps into the line to his right or left.
4. The linebackers move according to the movement of the coach.
5. The players return to their original positions and the drill is repeated.

Coaching Points

- In the beginning of the year, go one player at a time until you are confident that each player is looking at the ball and is moving correctly based on the movement of the ball.
- Make certain your linebackers move on the ball and adjust their charge correctly based on the ball movement.
- As each linebacker charges, his shoulders remain low and in position to take on a blocker. Both hands come up, with palms forward and fingers open as he starts his charge.
- When you move the ball to the inside, the IB on that side charges straight ahead while the other IB moves laterally to the side of the ball. The OB on the ball side steps across the line to be in position to take on a blocker, while the opposite OB pursues laterally to the ball.
- When you move the ball wide, the OB on the ball side crosses the line of scrimmage for two steps, to be in position to take on any blocker and also prepared to react down the line of scrimmage if the ball goes to his outside. The other linebackers pursue laterally to the side of the ball, staying inside the ball's movement.
- Make certain that each group of linebackers reacts properly to each of the four ball movements.

Defeating Run Blocks

When teaching linebackers the individual blocks they will have to defeat, get the players to work as partners, with each player reacting to the block, then moving over to play offensive blocker.

In the beginning, have the linebacker and the blocker go at half speed. These drills are designed to teach defensive players to react to a variety of blocks—not to create maximum contact.

It is important for you to decide what blocks your linebackers will face. In the beginning of the year, base your choices on your team's offense, then later in the year on your opponent's attack. Spend individual time teaching players how to defeat these blocks.

As you design your defense, tell each linebacker which gap is his primary responsibility. As he reacts to the various blocks, coach him to position his head on the side of his gap responsibility.

When first teaching block protection to your linebackers, have only one player go at a time.

Teaching the Order of Who Will Block the Player and How

Before actually learning the techniques, the players will need to learn the variety of blocks they will face. It is good to give them an understanding of who can block them and the type of block each offensive player can use. This is called block progression, and hopefully it will teach your defensive players how to anticipate and recognize what is happening as the ball is snapped.

Each defensive player has a natural progression to follow on every defensive play. This progression consists of:

1. Stepping forward on the center snap.
2. Discovering who is blocking you.
3. Recognizing the type of block being used.
4. Reacting to the block.
5. Defeating the blocker.
6. Locating and moving to the ball carrier.

🏈 LEARNING BLOCKERS

Number of players: All LBs
Equipment: Shorts or full pads
Time: 2 minutes/once a week

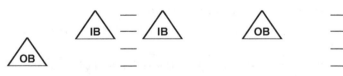
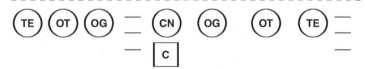

1. This is a mental drill and does not require movement.
2. Players simulating the offensive players are on one knee.
3. Defensive players are positioned based on the defensive front to be used.
4. The players on defense stand up so they can point out the order in which the blockers can attack them.

5. The coach points to each defensive player and has him point and call out the order of the blockers and state the type of block each will use.

6. Players move from offense to defense until every linebacker has gone through the drill.

Coaching Points

- For the OBs, playing in front of a TE, the read is TE first with a drive or hook block; OT second with a hook block.
- For the OBs playing in front of the OTs, the read is OT first with a drive or hook block; TE second with a down block; OG third with a hook block.
- For the IBs, playing in front of the OGs, the read is OG first with a drive or hook block; OT second with a down block; CN third with a hook block; TE fourth with a down block.
- For the IBs playing in front of the CN, the read is CN first with a drive or hook block; either OG on the side of the play second with a down block; either OG opposite the play third with a hook block; either OT fourth with a down block.
- For any OB playing outside the OT in space (off the line without a blocker in front of him), the read is OT first with a hook block; OG second with a drive or hook block.
- If your team is facing an opponent who uses an RB as a lead blocker, then this person should be added to the block progression reads of your linebackers.
- Emphasize to your linebackers that this is how they should be thinking prior to the start of each play.

Defeating the Run Blocks from the Player in Front of You

A linebacker must first anticipate a block by the blocker directly in front of him and be prepared to meet and defeat the block before locating the ball carrier.

🏈 DRIVE BLOCK PROTECTION

Number of players: All LBs
Equipment: Full pads, markers, ball
Time: 4 minutes/twice a week

1. All linebackers line up across the field at the proper depth—based on their position—facing the coach.

2. The coach tells the linebackers their gap responsibility—either right or left. (The diagram shows right.)

3. On the command of "Stance," each player on offense and defense gets into the appropriate stance for his position.

4. The linebackers focus on the ball.

5. On the command of "Hut," the CN makes the snap, and the blockers move forward to drive block the defensive player in front of them.

6. The linebacker reacts to the block (see below).

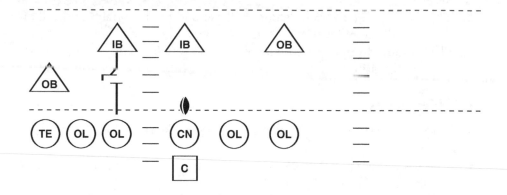

7. The coach calls out "Stop" or blows a whistle to stop the drill.

8. The offensive and defensive players change positions and repeat the drill.

Coaching Points

- Drive Block Protection:
    1. When the ball is snapped, the linebacker steps forward using short, powerful steps.
    2. As he comes forward, he keeps his shoulder pads under the pads of the offensive blocker.
    3. He brings both arms forward, hitting the blocker in the chest with the palms of both hands.
    4. As he makes contact, the linebacker slides his head to the side of his gap responsibility and extends his arms, getting separation from the blocker.
    5. He then attempts to shed the blocker opposite his gap responsibility or drive him back to the line of scrimmage.

HOOK BLOCK PROTECTION

Number of players: All LBs
Equipment: Full pads, ball
Time: 4 minutes/twice a week

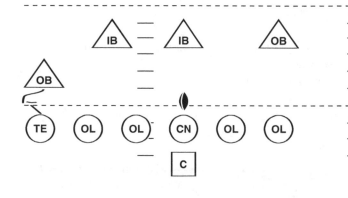

1. All linebackers line up across the field at the proper depth, based on their position, facing the coach.
2. The OB playing in front of the TE lines up on the outside shoulder of his opponent.
3. On command, each player on offense and defense gets into his stance.
4. The linebackers focus on the ball.
5. On the command of "Hut," the CN makes the snap, and each blocker moves forward to hook block the linebacker in front of him.
6. The linebacker reacts to the block (see below).
7. The coach calls out "Stop" or blows a whistle to stop the drill.
8. The offensive and defensive players change positions and repeat the drill.

Coaching Points

- Hook Block Protection
    1. As each offensive blocker starts his charge at the ball snap, the linebacker in front of him sees the head and upper body of the blocker moving to either his inside or outside (not driving straight ahead).
    2. When the linebacker sees this movement, he fires both hands straight ahead making contact with the shoulder pad and upper body of the blocker.
    3. He continues to extend his arms.
    4. At this point he creates separation from the blocker and drives the blocker down the line of scrimmage, keeping his head on the side of the blocker that is his gap responsibility.

Shedding a Run Block from the Side

In the two previous blocks, the linebacker was reacting to the blocker in front of him. This type of block (the drive or hook block) by an opposing offensive player is what your linebackers will face most of the time.

The next block your linebacker must recognize and learn to defeat is a block coming from his right or left from a second blocker. This is a *down* or *angle block* and usually comes from a blocker on the outside of the defensive lineman, although it may also come from a blocker lined up closer to the ball.

DOWN BLOCK PROTECTION

Number of players: All LBs
Equipment: Full pads, ball
Time: 4 minutes/twice a week

1. The linebackers form into three groups of three players, with space between each group.
2. The coach positions the linebackers based on the defensive front he plans to use.

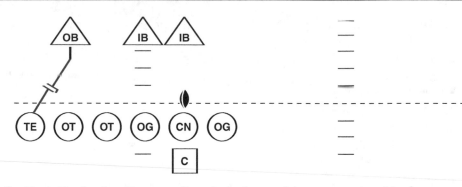

3. Each linebacker lines up directly in front of the appropriate blocker (OB↔OT, IB↔OG, and IB↔CN).
4. On the command of "Stance," the players on offense and defense get into their appropriate stances.
5. The linebackers focus on the ball.
6. On the command of "Hut," the CN makes the snap.
7. The blocker directly in front of the linebacker moves laterally away (to his right or left) from his offensive partner.
8. The other blocker down blocks on the linebacker.
9. The linebacker reacts to the block (see below).
10. The coach calls out "Stop" or blows a whistle to stop the drill.
11. The blocker and linebacker change positions. Repeat the drill until all three players have had their turn.
12. Set up the drill the next day with the linebackers on the other side of the ball.

Coaching Points

- Down Block Protection
    1. On the snap of the ball, the linebacker takes a short step straight ahead.
    2. When the linebacker sees that the player in front of him is not going to block him, he steps toward the blocker coming from his side.
    3. He stays low as he takes this short step.
    4. The linebacker meets the blocker with his shoulder pad and forearm on the side of the block.
    5. He then brings the palm of his other hand around making contact with the shoulder pads of the blocker.
- Emphasize to the linebacker that he needs to first stop the blocker, then hold his position, and finally shed the blocker.
- If the linebacker is able to get separation from the blocker, he should move laterally in pursuit to the outside on the defensive side of the line of scrimmage.

Reacting to Three Potential Blockers

As the season progresses and your defensive linemen are reacting properly to the drive, hook, and down blocks, you can create a drill where the defensive player has to look and react to all three blocks.

🏈 3-BLOCK PROTECTION

Number of players: All LBs
Equipment: Full pads, ball
Time: 4 minutes/once a week (later in the season)

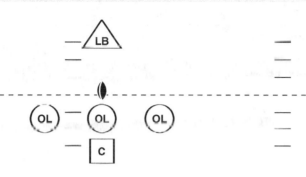

1. In this drill, the coach huddles up the three offensive players, designates the blocker and specifies the type of block to use.
2. The coach tells the LB his gap responsibility then gives the offensive players the snap count (1 or 2 hut) and brings them up to the line.
3. The ball is snapped on the coach's command and the block is executed.
4. The defensive player sees and reacts to defeat the offensive blocker.
5. The coach calls out "Stop" or blows a whistle to stop the drill.
6. The position of the ball can be moved to the right or left in relationship to the player's actual position.

Coaching Points

- This is a more advanced drill for your linebackers and should only be used when they know how to recognize and defeat each block individually.
- Make certain that the LB is reading the block and reacting appropriately.

Rushing the Passer

The next individual block your linebacker needs to react to is a *pass protection block*. This block is different because the blocker retreats off the line of scrimmage, not firing out on the snap of the ball. The challenge for the linebacker is to see and recognize the block as he comes on a *blitz* (rushing across the line on the snap) and to immediately attack toward the quarterback.

Prior to the start of the drill, mark the field where the quarterback will be setting up to throw. This marking gives your backers a target area to reach. You can adjust the position of each linebacker based on the alignment you are having him play on your defense.

In a game, a running back is often assigned to block an outside linebacker rushing from the outside, so this positioning should be incorporated into your drill. In this drill, rush men charge to the quarterback and blockers move back off the line, so for safety's sake have only one defensive rusher and one blocker go at a time.

🏈 TARGET RUSH

Number of players: All LBs
Equipment: Shorts or full pads, markers, blocking dummy (optional), ball
Time: 2 minutes/twice a week

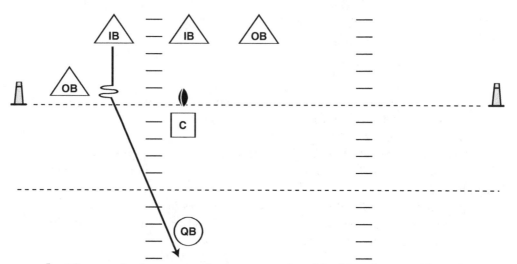

1. The coach places a marker, or a stand-up blocking dummy if one is available, directly behind the ball, 7 yards off the line of scrimmage to indicate the QB target area.
2. The coach informs each linebacker that this is the point they are sprinting to.
3. On the command of "Stance," the players assume their stance and look at the ball.
4. Once the players are set properly, the coach grasps the ball and simulates a snap (by pulling the ball toward him). The players charge up the field toward the QB target area, shorten their stride for three or four steps at the line of scrimmage, then sprint to the target.
5. The players return to their original positions and repeat the drill.

Coaching Points

- Make certain the players step forward on the snap.
- Target Rush:
   1. The linebacker's initial charge is straight to the line of scrimmage as he moves toward the QB target.

2. Both hands come up, with palms forward and fingers open as each linebacker starts his charge.
3. Players have their heads up and eyes open, with their arms moving in a normal running action as they continue across the line.
4. The linebackers continue running past the QB target area.

Basic Pass Rush Techniques

Once your linebackers are charging across the line and taking a proper path to the quarterback area, you can teach them basic pass rush techniques. Explain to your linebackers the numerous ways they can influence the opponents passing attack. They can:

1. Force the passer to throw before he is ready.
2. Reach up and deflect a pass, changing the path of the ball.
3. Tackle the quarterback before he has a chance to pass.
4. Make an interception.

Any one of these actions will greatly help your pass defense.

The linebacker reacts to the block against him when he is playing in his normal position on running plays. The offense knows where the ball is going to be run. The initial advantage is slanted to the offense.

This changes when an offensive blocker sets back to a pass protection block. Now the blitzing linebacker is the one who decides where and how he will rush the quarterback. The offense must react to his charge and movements. If the linebacker knows ahead of the snap how and where he is going to rush, the advantage shifts to the defensive player.

BULL PASS RUSH

Number of players: All LBs
Equipment: Shorts or full pads, markers, ball
Time: 3 minutes/twice a week

1. The coach designates the linebacker and blocker to run the drill.
2. Prior to starting the drill, the linebacker locates the spot where the QB will set up.
3. The linebacker pictures rushing through the blocker to the QB spot.
4. The CN snaps the ball on the command of "Hut," and the blocker sets up to pass protect.
5. The linebacker watches the ball snap, begins his blitz, and sees the offensive blocker setting up for a pass.
6. Once the linebacker has pushed the blocker back to the target area, the coach calls out "Stop" or blows a whistle to stop the drill.
7. The rush man changes position with the player on offense.

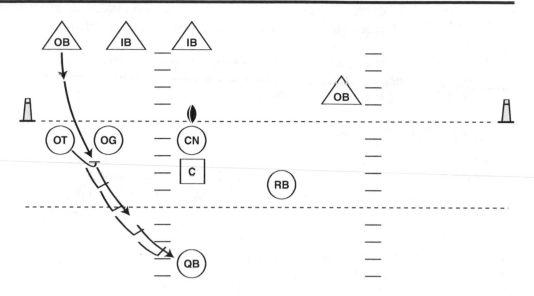

8. The coach has the next two players do the drill.

9. The drill is set up on the opposite side for the next run through.

Coaching Points

- When first teaching pass rush technique, have the linebacker rush at half speed.
- Make certain the linebacker steps forward on the snap.
- Bull Pass Rush:
  1. The linebacker's initial charge is straight toward the line of scrimmage.
  2. As he nears the blocker, he shortens his stride, lowers his hips, and continues to move forward.
  3. Both his hands come up, with palms forward and fingers open as he nears the blocker.
  4. His head is up and eyes are open.
  5. When he is close enough to touch the blocker, the linebacker drives the palms of both hands under the shoulder pads of the blocker.
  6. As his hands make contact with the armpit area of the blocker, he extends his arms, creating separation, pushing up and back as drives his legs in short choppy steps.
- Emphasize to the linebacker that his goal is to push the offensive blocker straight back into the QB target.

The bull rush is one of the easiest pass rush techniques to learn and is aided by the natural backward movement of the offensive blocker. The pass rusher should be taught to anticipate and expect the blocker to take a stand (stop his backward movement and lunge forward) once the offensive blocker has been pushed back into the quarterback. When this happens the defensive rusher must be ready to use the jerk rush to get past the blocker and move to the quarterback target area.

JERK PASS RUSH

Number of players: All LBs
Equipment: Shorts or full pads, ball
Time: 3 minutes/twice a week

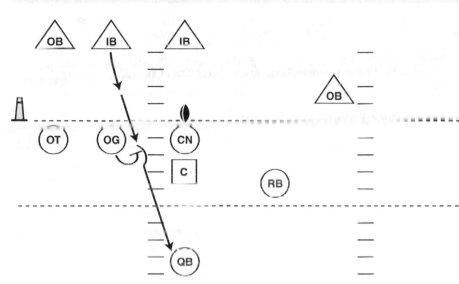

1. The coach designates which linebacker and blocker are to run the drill.
2. Prior to starting the drill, have the linebacker locate the spot where the QB will set up.
3. The linebacker pictures rushing around the blocker on the designated side to the QB spot.
4. The coach designates the side of the blocker (right or left) he wants the rusher to go.
5. The CN snaps the ball on the command of "Hut" and the blocker sets up to pass protect.
6. The linebacker watches the ball snap, begins his blitz, and sees the offensive blocker setting up for a pass.
7. The offensive lineman stops his backward movement and lunges forward when the linebacker nears him.
8. Once the linebacker is past the blocker the coach calls out "Stop" or blows a whistle to end the drill.
9. The rush man changes position with the player on offense.
10. The next two players do the drill.
11. The drill can be done from the other side on the next day.

Coaching Points

- When first teaching pass rush technique, have the linebacker rush at half speed.
- Make certain the linebacker steps forward on the snap.

- Jerk Pass Rush:
  1. The linebacker's initial charge is straight toward the line of scrimmage.
  2. As he nears the blocker, he shortens his stride, lowers his hips, and continues to move forward.
  3. The linebacker has his head up and eyes open.
  4. The linebacker reaches out with both hands and grabs the blocker's jersey when he sees the blocker setting up and lunging forward.
  5. The linebacker uses the forward lunge of the blocker to pull blocker to the opposite side that he is going to rush (rush left—pull right; rush right—pull left).
  6. The linebacker steps across the blocker's body with the leg and foot on the side to which he is jerking the blocker. This allows the linebacker to get clear of the block.
  7. The linebacker sprints to the QB target area once he is past the blocker.

Teaching Pass Coverage to Linebackers

Another basic set of skills to teach your linebackers is pass coverage. Start by teaching man-to-man techniques and then teaching zone techniques.

The man-to-man techniques are used by your linebackers in moving to their zone coverage. Even though you may be featuring zone pass coverage, sometimes you will want to blitz, and your linebackers will be forced to play man coverage. So it is important for them to know the correct technique.

🏈 BACKWARD START

Number of players: All LBs
Equipment: Shorts or full pads
Time: 2 minutes/every day

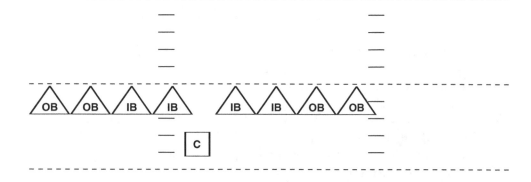

1. All linebackers line up across the field facing the coach.
2. On the command of "Stance," each player gets into his proper stance.
3. The coach scans down the line checking that everyone is properly set.

4. On the command of "Hut," each player takes two or three steps straight back (see below).
5. After making their start, the players line up again and repeat the drill.

Coaching Points

- In the beginning of the season, go one player at a time until you are confident that each player understands how to start correctly.
- Each linebacker pushes off his inside front foot and takes a short step back with his outside foot while pushing his hips back.
- All linebackers step back with their first step, keeping their shoulders in front of their hips as they get started.

🏈 BACKWARD RUN

Number of players: All LBs
Equipment: Shorts or full pads, markers
Time: 2 minutes/every day

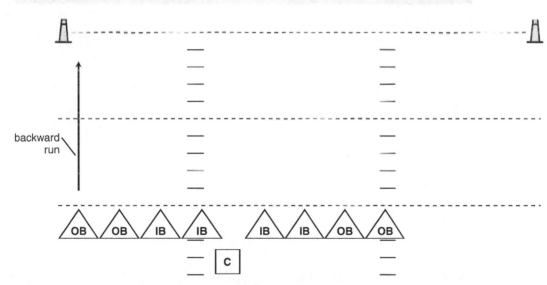

1. All form a line across the field facing the coach.
2. On the command of "Stance," each player gets into his proper stance.
3. The coach scans down the line checking that everyone is properly set.
4. On the command of "Hut," each linebacker runs backward for 10 yards.
5. The players line up again and repeat the drill.

Coaching Points

- In the beginning of the season, go one player at a time until you are confident that each player understands how to backpedal correctly.

- For a Backpedal, players:
  1. Step backward with each step.
  2. Have their shoulders in front of their hips, their heads up, and their arms moving in a natural running motion.

🏈 FORWARD RUN

Number of players: All LBs
Equipment: Shorts or full pads, markers
Time: 3 minutes/every day

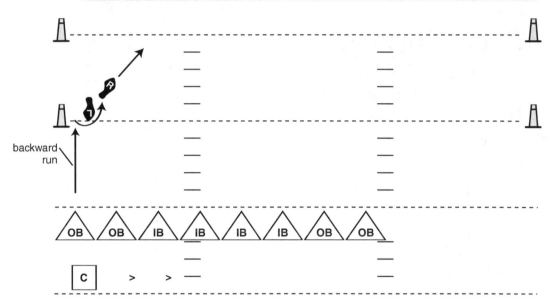

1. All linebackers form a line across the field facing the coach.
2. At first the coach moves down the line with one player going at a time, then all players can go right or left, based on the coach's call at 5 yards.
3. On the command of "Stance," each linebacker gets into his proper stance.
4. On the command of "Hut," each linebacker starts and runs straight back for 5 yards.
5. When a player nears 5 yards, the coach points deep right or left, indicating the direction the linebacker is to turn and run forward.
6. The linebacker continues his forward run for 5 yards before returning to his starting spot.

Coaching Points

- Be sure each player has the chance to go deep to his right and left.

- For a Forward Run, the player:
   1. Leans his upper body in the direction he plans to go.
   2. Plants the foot on that side of his body and brings the opposite leg across his body in a natural motion to pivot and take his first forward step.
   3. Keeps his feet under his hips as he runs and maintains his momentum throughout the drill. This will keep him from slipping on a wet surface or stopping and starting again when he goes into his forward run.

Dropping for Zone Coverage

To play good zone pass defense, linebackers must know where the zones are located and know the quickest way to move to their assigned zone.

When first teaching zones, mark the ground with chalk, a cone, or a piece of cloth. This gives the linebacker a reference point for each zone, and in the later drill, a definitive area to work toward in his drop. The actual zone he is assigned to will depend on the zone coverage you plan to teach (*2-deep zone* or *3-deep zone*).

NAMING THE LINEBACKER ZONES

Number of players: All LBs
Time: 2 minutes/twice a week (beginning of season)

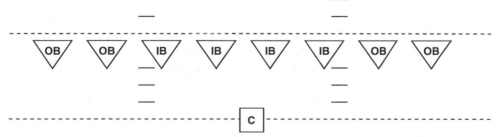

1. All linebackers line up spread out across the field with their backs to the coach.
2. Each player points and calls out the zones in his area of the field.

3. Once each player knows the name of every zone and has an idea of its location, you can eliminate this drill.

Coaching Points

- The QBs need to know the name and location of the hook and out zones on their side of the ball.
- The IBs need to know the name and location of the hook and center zones on both sides of the ball.

ZONE DROPS

Number of players: All LBs
Equipment: Shorts or full pads
Time: 4 minutes/twice a week

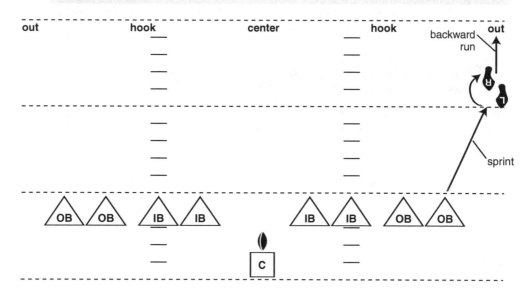

1. All linebackers line up across the field facing the coach.
2. On the command of "Stance," each player gets into his proper stance.
3. The coach slaps the ball, and each player moves to his assigned zone based on the defense that's been called and sets up.
4. The coach raises the ball as a signal to the linebacker to stop his backward run and move in the direction of the pass.
5. Players return to their original positions and repeat the drill.

Coaching Points

- In the beginning of the season, move down the line and have one player at a time drop into a designated zone. Then have all players go to their proper zone based on the defense called. When the linebackers move as a unit they will see the relationship they have with one another and the distance between their assigned positions.

- When a linebacker needs a wider stride to reach his assigned zone, have him take his normal step back, then pivot on the foot that's closer to the direction he needs to go and sprint to his zone.
- Once the linebacker reaches his zone, he must swing his inside leg around and go into his backward run.
- When a linebacker does not need to widen his stride to reach his zone, he can use his backward run during the entire drop, or he can take a few sprint steps, then swing around into his backward run.
- All linebackers must focus on the coach and the ball.
- When the coach raises the ball to a passing position, the linebackers stop moving backward and use a chop step movement maintaining that position.
- When the coach sees the linebackers under control, he steps to a point on the field and goes through a simulated passing motion.
- As the coach steps to throw, every linebacker should pivot on the foot that's in the direction of the throw and sprint to that spot.

Running Back Drills

Playing an offensive back position requires a variety of skills. At different times during the game, a running back will be asked to carry the ball, block for another runner, carry out a fake, run a pass route, become a receiver, and help protect the quarterback when he is dropping back to pass.

Mentally the running backs must understand the offense, know what hole to hit, and have a general idea of what the defense is trying to do.

There are basic drills you can use that do not require the addition of another player. These drills will focus on skills that the running backs can work on to develop their individual techniques.

2-, 4-, 3-POINT STANCE

Number of players: All RBs
Equipment: Shorts or full pads
Time: 2 minutes/every day

1. All running backs line up across the field facing the coach.
2. The coach indicates which stance he wants the players to assume, and on the command of "Stance," each player gets into that stance.
3. The coach scans down the line checking that everyone is properly set.
4. On the command of "Up," players come out of their stance to an upright position.

Coaching Points

- In the beginning of the season, the coach should go one player at a time until he is confident that each player understands his stance.
- Only teach running backs the stances they will use in your offense.
- Have every running back (HBs and FBs) stand upright, feet even and spread hip width.

Running back 2-point stance.

- Start with the 2-Point Stance:
  1. On the command of "Stance," each running back bends his knees and places the palms of both hands on the inside of each thigh just above the knee joint, with the thumbs of both hands on the inside of the thighs.
  2. His shoulders and head are slightly ahead of the hips, with his back straight, head up, and eyes looking straight ahead.
  3. The running back's weight is evenly distributed on the balls of both feet, with his knees slightly flexed.
- Next have the running backs get into a 4-Point Stance:
  1. Each running back assumes his 2-point stance, then adjusts both arms so that his forearms rest on either thigh.
  2. From this position he reaches straight forward with both arms and places the fingertips of both hands on the ground slightly ahead of his shoulder pads.
  3. In this position, hips and shoulders are even, with his back straight, head up, and eyes straight ahead.
- Last, call out the 3-Point Stance:
  1. Each running back assumes his 4-point stance.
  2. From this position, he lifts one hand off the ground and places that forearm on his thigh.
  3. Shoulders should remain even.
- In a 3-point stance, the running back should have little weight on the down hand (the hand on the ground) so that he can move laterally as well as straight ahead.

🏈 START

Number of players: All RBs
Equipment: Shorts or full pads
Time: 2 minutes/every day

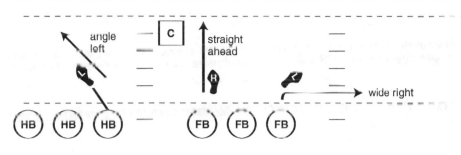

1. All running backs line up across the field facing the coach.
2. The coach indicates which stance he wants the players to assume, and on the command of "Stance," each player gets into his proper stance.
3. The coach calls out the direction he wants the players to start: straight ahead; angle right or left; or wide right or left
4. On the command of "Hut," each player starts properly and takes three or four steps in the correct direction.
5. After making their start, the players line up again and repeat the drill.

Coaching Points

- In the beginning of the season, observe one player at a time until you're confident that each player understands how to start correctly.
- Vary the stance based on your offense and the direction of the start during the drill.
- Have each running back assume the designated stance.
- Make certain that running backs take a short directional step with the outside foot when they are starting straight ahead or take a short directional step with the foot on the side of their charge when they are starting at an angle (left foot: angle left; right foot: angle right).
- When starting wide to either side, players should lean in that direction and pivot on the foot on that side as they start bringing their other leg across their body to turn wide.
- They should keep their forward lean, gaining ground with each step, and swing their arms in a normal running action.
- Head and eyes should be focused on the direction they are going.

Ball Protection and Running Drills

One of the first lessons a running back needs to learn is that he must protect the ball. It is important that he grasp the ball correctly and cover the ball with both hands if he is about to be hit by defensive players.

RB Ball Protection

To emphasize the importance of holding onto the ball, set up a drill where the other running backs try to dislodge the ball from the running back holding the ball.

BALL PROTECTION

Number of players: All RBs
Equipment: Shorts or full pads
Time: 2 minutes/every day

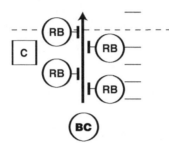

1. The ball carrier (BC) faces up the field with the ball in either his right or left hand.
2. On the command of "Hut," the BC starts up the field and runs between the two lines of RBs.
3. As he runs through the two lines, the other RBs reach out to try to dislodge the ball without actually tackling the BC.
4. When the BC reaches the end of the line, he gives the ball to the coach and takes the place of the last man in line, and everyone moves up.
5. The coach throws the ball to the first man in line who then takes his place as BC and repeats the drill.
6. Each day alternate the arms that the BC uses to hold the ball.

Coaching Points

- Check that the BC has the ball securely in his grasp prior to starting his run: the palm of his hand is over the front tip of the ball, the ball is secured at his side with his forearm, and the back point of the ball is tucked into his armpit.
- As he runs the BC keeps the ball snugly in place against his body.
- If the BC feels the ball being dislodged, he quickly brings the front point of the ball across his stomach and grasps the back point of the ball with the palm of his other hand.
- When he has the ball grasped in both hands, the forearm with the hand on the back point of the ball will be across the top of the ball, and the other forearm will be on the underside of the ball.

Avoiding the Tackler

More often than not your young running backs will either run into tacklers or have the speed to run away from them. Even with a beginning running back, it is good to teach them a third option: making the tackler miss. The first technique that I suggest you teach your running back is a crossover step technique to avoid the tackler.

CROSSOVER STEP

Number of players: All RBs
Equipment: Shorts or full pads, markers, ball
Time: 1 minutes/once a week

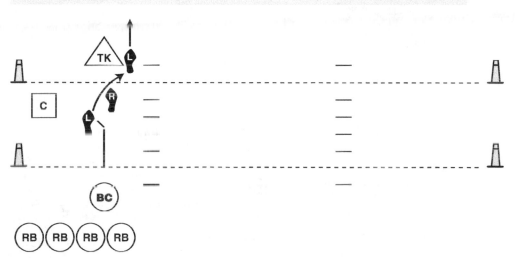

1. The BC lines up 6 yards away from the tackler (TK).
2. The coach designates to the BC the direction of his crossover step.
3. The BC carries the ball in his hand on the side of his cut (direction he will go to avoid the TK).
4. On the command of "Hut," the BC starts up the field and runs toward the TK.
5. The TK steps forward but does not try to tackle, and the BC executes the crossover step (see below).
6. The BC gives the ball to the TK, who runs it to the next BC and goes to the end of the RB line to wait his turn. The former BC becomes the next TK.
7. The coach starts the drill again for the next BC.

Coaching Points

- It may be necessary to have the BC go at half speed in the beginning so that he gets the steps and body positions correct.
- Run the drill to both sides of the TK.

- Crossover Step (for movement to the right):
  1. When the BC is about three steps away from the TK, he starts the maneuver by taking a short step with his left foot to the outside of the TK.
  2. He then takes a second step with his right foot directly at the TK as he makes a quick fake with his head to the left.
  3. He leans his upper body to the right as his right foot hits the ground.
  4. From this position, he quickly brings his left leg completely across in front of his body to change the direction and path of his run.
- The BC should lean his upper body to make it easier to bring his leg across the front of his body and make the defender miss.
- When the BC goes to the left, he has the ball in his left hand and he uses the opposite steps and body lean to complete the maneuver.

Knowing Where to Run

It is important for running backs to identify the running lanes, or holes. Teams have different ways of indicating the holes, but the most common is having the even-numbered holes to the right of the offensive center and the odd-numbered holes to the left of the offensive center. Generally, the larger the number of the hole, the farther it is from the offensive center.

🏈 HOLE NUMBERING

Number of players: All RBs
Equipment: Shorts or full pads, markers
Time: 4 minutes/once a week

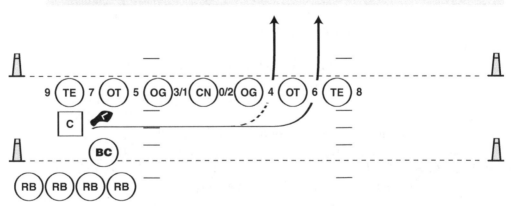

1. The coach marks the ground to indicate the locations of the five offensive linemen (CN, OGs, OTs) and the two TEs.
2. The coach explains how the running lanes (holes) are numbered and that the opening will occur between the offensive blockers.
3. RBs line up one at a time.
4. The coach calls out the hole that he wants the BC to attack.

5. On the command of "Hut," the BC attacks the proper hole and runs up the field for 10 yards.

6. Once the BC has executed his maneuver, he takes a place at the end of the RB line.

7. Have each BC start from both sides of the ball.

Coaching Points

- If the BC is attacking a running lane on his side of the ball, make certain he starts with a short directional step with his foot on the side of the hole

- If he is attacking a hole on the other side of the offensive CN (as shown in the diagram), he starts with a crossover step with his outside foot to get his body turned in the proper direction.

- Emphasize to each BC that he should run laterally if he is attacking a hole on the other side of the center, then pivot on his inside foot at the last minute as he is cutting into the hole that's been called.

- When a BC is attacking a wide hole (8 or 9 hole) on the side of his original alignment, he starts with a crossover step with his inside foot to get his body quickly turned to the outside. This type of start is used on a play where the QB is going to pitch or toss the ball back to the RB and not hand it off.

Blocking on Running Plays

In addition to carrying the ball on running plays, one of the running backs may be required to block for the ball carrier. Often this block will be right at the point of attack (where the ball is to be run). In most cases, a block by a running back happens while the running back is on the move, and he will run a distance before he reaches the defensive player, usually a linebacker.

In many cases the defensive player may be larger than your blocker. So it is important that you instruct him to attack only one side of the defensive man, to block with his shoulder pad and forearm, and to always have his head up and eyes open as he makes contact and slides his head to one side or the other of the defensive man's body.

🏈 LEAD BLOCKING FOR THE RUN

Number of players: All RBs
Equipment: Shorts or full pads, markers, blocking shield or a lightweight blocking dummy
Time: 5 minutes/once a week

1. The coach marks the field to indicate the locations of the five offensive linemen (CN, OGs, OTs) and the two TEs.

2. One running back lines up as an IB on the side of the RB who is going to block.

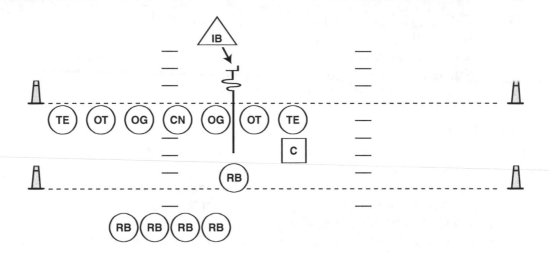

3. The player lining up on defense has a handheld blocking shield or a lightweight stand-up blocking dummy that the blocker can safely attack.

4. One RB lines up at a time.

5. The coach calls out to the defensive player the direction he wants him to move during the drill.

6. On the command of "Hut," the RB attacks the defensive man and blocks him for four or five steps (see below).

7. Once the RB has executed his maneuver, he takes the place of the defensive man, and the defensive man goes to the end of the RB line.

Coaching Points

- Have each blocker line up and block from both sides of the ball.
- Have each RB execute the drill with the IB in front of the OG and OT position.
- If your offense requires the lead back to block from a position directly behind the offensive center, make sure that you do this at some point in this drill.
- Emphasize to each RB that the quicker he gets to the defensive player the better, and that he must focus on the defender he is blocking.
- Lead Block for the Run:
    1. As the RB nears the defensive man, he shortens and widens his stride keeping his shoulders slightly in front of his hips.
    2. He keeps his hips over his feet and bends his knees as he gets ready to make contact.
    3. The RB focuses only on blocking one side of the defensive man, aiming at one hip.
    4. The RB drives his shoulder and forearm at the defender's hip while driving his legs.
    5. He drives off the foot on the side of his body that he is using to block the defensive player.
    6. His head is up and eyes are open as he blocks, and his head slides to the side of the defensive man.
- When the RB is asked to *lead block* on an IB and the play starts, he may not know which way he is going to block the defensive man and which shoulder to use to block. Therefore:
    - The RB should focus on the linebacker's numbers and take a path directly at the linebacker.
    - The RB lets the linebacker choose the side, then blocks the linebacker in that direction.

- In a game, the BC watches the RB's lead block and cuts to the opposite side of his block.
- Make certain that the RB blocks with the same technique—shoulder pad to the hip area—once he determines the direction of the linebacker's movement.

Blocking an Outside Linebacker

The running back may also be asked to block an outside linebacker to the outside on off-tackle plays or to the inside on wide running plays. The path the running back takes to the linebacker should be the same for both blocks. The difference between the two blocks is the running back's target area. If the running back is blocking the linebacker to the outside (*kickout block*), the running back hits the linebacker's inside hip area. When the running back is blocking the linebacker to the inside (*hook block*), he should contact the linebacker's outside hip. On both blocks, the running back focuses on the target area and makes good contact with his shoulder pad and forearm.

🏈 KICKOUT BLOCKING FOR THE RUN

Number of players: All RBs

Equipment: Shorts or full pads, markers, blocking shield or a lightweight blocking dummy

Time: 5 minutes/once a week

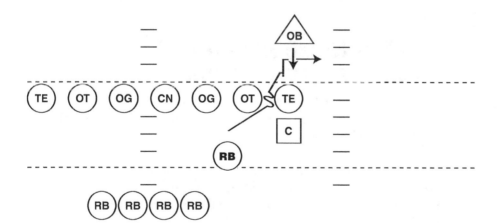

1. The coach marks the ground to indicate the locations of the five offensive linemen (CN, OGs, OTs) and the two TEs.
2. One running back lines up as an OB on the side of the RB who is going to block.
3. The player lining up on defense uses a handheld blocking shield or a lightweight stand-up blocking dummy that the RB can safely attack.
4. Have one RB line up at a time.

5. On the command of "Hut," the RB attacks the defensive man and blocks him for four or five steps (see below).

6. Once the RB executes this maneuver, he takes the place of the defensive man, and the defensive man goes to the end of the RB line.

Coaching Points

- Have each RB line up and block from both sides of the ball.
- If your offense requires the lead back to block from a position directly behind the offensive center, make sure you do this at some point in this drill.
- Emphasize to each RB that the quicker he gets to the defender the better and that he must focus on the defender he is blocking.
- Kickout Blocking for the Run:
    1. As the RB nears the defensive man, he shortens and widens his stride, keeping his shoulders slightly in front of his hips.
    2. He keeps his hips over his feet, bending his knees as he gets ready to make contact.
    3. The RB focuses only on blocking one side of the defensive man, aiming at the inside hip of the defender.
    4. The RB drives his outside shoulder and forearm at the defender's inside hip, driving with his legs.
    5. He drives off his outside foot as his shoulder pad makes contact.
    6. His head is up and eyes are open as he blocks, and his head slides to the inside of the defensive man.
    7. The RB finishes the block by driving the OB out toward the sideline.

🏈 HOOK BLOCKING FOR THE RUN

Number of players: All RBs
Equipment: Shorts or full pads, markers, blocking shield or a lightweight blocking dummy
Time: 5 minutes/once a week

1. The coach marks the ground to indicate the locations of the five offensive linemen (CN, OGs, OTs) and the two TEs.

2. One running back lines up as an OB on the side of the RB who is going to block.

3. The player lining up on defense has a handheld blocking shield or a lightweight stand-up blocking dummy that the RB can safely attack.

4. One RB lines up at a time.

5. On the command of "Hut," the RB attacks the defensive man and blocks him for four or five steps (see below).

6. Once the RB has executed his maneuver, he takes the place of the defensive man, and the defensive man can go to the end of the running back line.

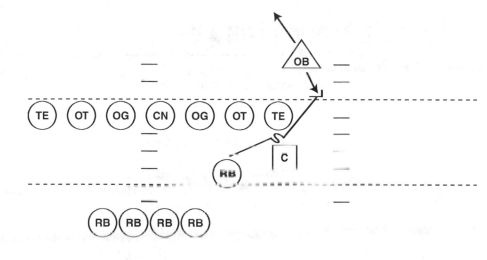

7. Have each RB line up and block from both sides of the ball.

Coaching Points

- If your offense requires the lead back to block from a position directly behind the offensive center, make sure that you do this at some point in this drill.
- Emphasize to each RB that the sooner he gets to the defensive player the better, that he must focus on the defender he is blocking, and that his path to the backer should be identical to the path used in the Kickout Blocking drill (see page 101).
- Hook Blocking for the Run:
  1. As the RB nears the defensive man, he shortens and widens his stride, keeping his shoulders slightly in front of his hips.
  2. He keeps his hips over his feet, bending his knees as he gets ready to make contact.
  3. The RB focuses only on blocking one side of the defensive man, aiming at the outside hip of the defender.
  4. The RB drives his inside shoulder and forearm at the defender's outside hip, driving with his legs.
  5. He drives off his inside foot as his shoulder pad makes contact.
  6. His head is up and eyes are open as he blocks, and his head slides to the outside of the defensive man.
  7. The RB finishes the block by driving the OB back and in toward the center of the field.

Blocking Downfield

Often a running back will be asked to block a defensive back who may be coming up toward the line of scrimmage or staying back in the defensive backfield as the play develops. The running back should use the same technique that he used on the kickout block except that he now has to locate the defensive back and determine how the defensive back is going to react during the play.

🏈 KICKOUT BLOCKING ON A DB

Number of players: All RBs
Equipment: Shorts or full pads, markers, blocking shield
Time: 5 minutes/once a week

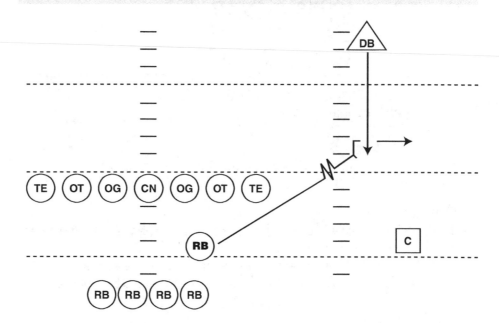

1. The coach marks the ground to indicate the locations of the five offensive linemen (CN, OGs, OTs) and the two TEs.
2. One running back lines up as a DB on the side of the RB who is going to block.
3. The player lining up on defense uses a handheld blocking shield that the RB can safely attack.
4. One RB lines up at a time.
5. The coach indicates to the DB if he should come up or stay back during the drill.
6. When first teaching the block, tell the RB how the DB is going to react.
7. Once the RB is comfortable in finding the DB and blocking him, regardless of his reaction, run the drill without alerting the RB to the DB's reaction.
8. On the command of "Hut," the RB starts correctly, attacks the DB, and blocks him for four or five steps (see below).
9. Once the RB has executed his maneuver, he takes the place of the DB, and the DB moves to the end of the RB line.
10. Each RB lines up and blocks from both sides of the ball.

Coaching Points

- If your offense requires the RB to block from a position directly behind the offensive CN, make sure that you do this at some point during this blocking drill.
- Emphasize to each RB the quicker he gets to the defensive back, the easier his block will be, and that he must locate and focus on the defender he is blocking.
- If the DB is coming up, the RB must anticipate his path and adjust his own path to intersect the defensive player.
- Kickout Blocking on a DB:
    1. As the RB nears the DB, he shortens and widens his stride, keeping his shoulders slightly in front of his hips.
    2. He keeps his hips over his feet, bending his knees as he gets ready to make contact.
    3. The RB focuses on blocking one side of the defensive man, aiming at the inside hip of the defender.
    4. The RB drives his outside shoulder and forearm at the defender's inside hip, driving with his legs.
    5. He must drive off his outside foot as his shoulder pad makes contact.
    6. His head is up and eyes are open as he blocks, and his head slides to the inside of the defensive man.
    7. The RB finishes the block by driving the DB out toward the sideline.
- When the DB stays back and does not attack the line of scrimmage, the RB should anticipate the DB moving to the right or left at the last moment.
- The RB heads directly at the DB and uses the same technique he used for a lead block on an IB (see Lead Blocking for the Run, page 100).
- It is important for the RB to focus on the DB's numbers as the RB turns up the field and takes a path directly at the DB.
- The RB lets the DB choose a side, then blocks the DB in that direction.
- He blocks the DB either inside or outside, based on the direction of the DB's movement, and knows that the BC will cut to the opposite direction.

Taking the Handoff

Any skill and ability that running backs have as ball carriers starts with the handoff. In a game, it is the quarterback's job to put the ball firmly into the running back's pocket. The ball carrier needs to understand that it is his responsibility to secure the ball in his grasp for the remainder of the play.

Running back ready to receive handoff.

🏈 HANDOFF

Number of players: All RBs
Equipment: Shorts or full pads, markers, ball
Time: 3 minutes/once a week early in year

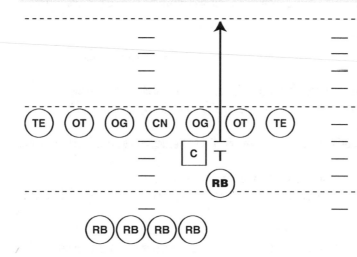

1. The coach marks the ground to indicate the locations of the five offensive linemen (CN, OGs, OTs) and the two TEs.
2. One RB starts and receives the handoff.
3. The coach calls out "Hut" to start the drill.
4. The RB starts straight ahead and receives the ball from the coach.
5. The RB runs 5 yards, returns the ball to the coach, and proceeds to the end of the line.
6. The coach has the next RB in line execute the drill.
7. The drill is run both to the left and right of the CN.

Coaching Points

- The Handoff:
  1. The RB forms a pocket with his two hands to receive the ball.
  2. One arm (the arm closest to the coach) is above his stomach while the other arm extends below the stomach.
  3. The RB places his upper arm in the same position each time, with his elbow positioned just below his shoulder.
  4. The forearm of his top arm, from his elbow to wrist, should be across his chest.
  5. The palm of his hand on the top arm needs to be angled down so that it can quickly engulf the point of the ball.

6. The RB positions his bottom arm to form the pocket when receiving the handoff.
7. The forearm of his bottom arm should be slightly below and across his stomach.
8. The palm of the hand is turned up slightly to grasp the ball.
9. As you place the ball in the RB's pocket, he secures the ball with both hands.
10. He quickly lowers his upper hand and forearm and raises his lower hand and forearm, clasping the ball tightly.

- At the beginning of the season, have the RBs keep two arms on the ball during the drill.
- Once the season starts, the quarterback and the running back will be working on making and securing the ball during handoffs and this drill may be eliminated. Keep an eye on the exchange of the ball and make certain that each running back is forming a good pocket and is securing the ball immediately after the handoff.

Learning Pass Routes

Basic Pass Routes

The following running back drills focus on the basic pass routes (or pass patterns). The patterns you feature depend on the passing ability of your quarterback, the ability of your offensive line to pass protect, and the receiving ability of your running backs. Spend a majority of your time in practice throwing the passes that you anticipate using in a game.

Pass routes are usually broken down by the distance the receiver runs off the line before executing his pass pattern. The three general areas are *short* (up to 4 yards), *medium* (around 8 yards), and *deep* (over 8 yards down the field). If your field is not lined, set up markers—cones, flags, or shirts—at the depth of the pattern to give the receivers a point of reference for making their break.

Each pass route must be coordinated with the drop of the quarterback for the ball to be delivered on time to the receiver. It is vital that your receivers run each route at the proper depth and be in position to make the catch when the quarterback is ready to deliver the ball.

Because a running back is often lined up 4 yards in the backfield, the quarterback often takes five steps before delivering the ball even for short pass routes. On medium and deep routes, the quarterback will definitely drop back five steps.

Leave the ball out of the drill when teaching your running backs to run each pass route correctly. Without the ball, the emphasis is on learning how to run the pass pattern and not worrying about making the catch. The running back starts at the line of scrimmage exactly the same way regardless of the pass route that he is going to run.

The two basic short routes are *flat* and *angle*.

🏈 SHORT PASS ROUTES

Number of players: All RBs
Equipment: Shorts or full pads, markers
Time: 2 minutes/once a week

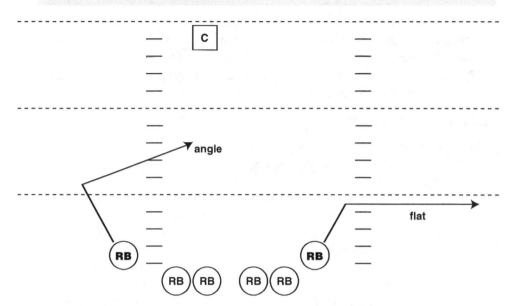

1. The first player in each group lines up in his RB stance and listens for the coach's call on the pass route (flat or angle).
2. On the command of "Hut," both RBs run the pattern called (see below).
3. After the pattern has been run, the two RBs go to the back of the line, and the next two RBs step up and get into their stance.
4. Each RB runs each pattern to both sides of the field.

Coaching Points

- In the beginning, the players may need to go one at a time.
- Flat Route:
    1. The RB starts toward the line of scrimmage at a 45-degree angle outside of where his OT would normally be.
    2. Once he reaches the line of scrimmage, he pivots on his outside foot and breaks directly toward the sideline.
    3. He continues to run to the outside of the field.
- Angle Route:
    1. The RB aims for the same spot on his start as on the flat route.
    2. When he reaches the line of scrimmage, he breaks at a 45-degree angle back into the center of the field instead of flat to the sideline.
- On both pass routes, it is important that he quickly turns his head back to the QB and has his hands ready to make the catch.

- In a game, the RB must be prepared to catch the ball at any height and may need to adjust his path to make the catch.

MEDIUM PASS ROUTES

Number of players: All RBs
Equipment: Shorts or full pads, markers
Time: 2 minutes/once a week

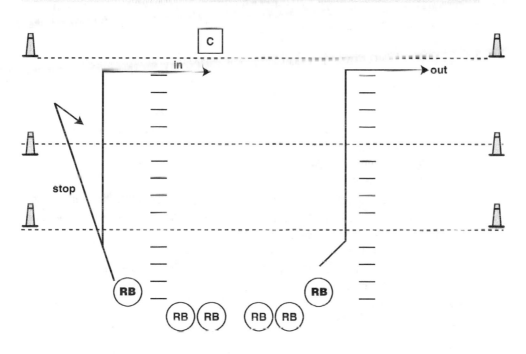

Once the running backs have learned the two short pass routes you can teach them the three medium pass routes: *stop, out,* and *in.* A medium pass pattern is run in an area 8 yards across the line of scrimmage. The running back runs 11 to 15 yards before making his final break to catch the ball, so he should run as fast as he can to give the quarterback enough time to throw him the ball. For maximum success, the running back should give the defensive men the feeling that he is going to run deep up the field.

1. The first player in each group lines up in his RB stance and listens for the coach to call out the pass route (stop, in, or out).
2. On the command of "Hut," both RBs run the pattern called (see below).
3. The players running the pattern go to the back of the line, and the next two RBs step up and get into their stance.
4. Each RB runs each pattern to both sides of the field.

Coaching Points

- In the beginning, the players may need to go one at a time.
- On all three medium pass routes, the RB starts toward the line of scrimmage at a 45-degree angle outside his offensive tackle.
- Stop Route:
  1. The RB starts toward the line of scrimmage at a 45-degree angle outside his offensive tackle.
  2. As he continues on this path, he aims for a point 7 yards across the line of scrimmage and 8 yards outside the OT.
  3. He shortens his stride and gets his feet under his hips, lowering his hips when he nears this spot.
  4. He stops his forward movement by planting his outside foot and turning quickly back to the inside.
  5. As he makes his turn, he snaps his head around, bringing both hands up in a position to make the catch.
- In Route:
  1. The RB starts toward the line of scrimmage at a 45-degree angle outside his offensive tackle.
  2. He turns up the field the instant he reaches the line of scrimmage, pivots on his inside foot at 8 yards, and breaks straight across the center of the field.
  3. He turns his head back to the QB the minute he makes his break.
- Out Route:
  1. The RB starts toward the line of scrimmage at a 45-degree angle outside his offensive tackle.
  2. He turns up the field the instant he reaches the line of scrimmage, pivots on his outside foot at 8 yards, and breaks to the sideline.
  3. He turns his head back to the QB the minute he makes his break.
- Be sure to alert the RB that he may have to bend back to the line of scrimmage to make the catch because of the distance the ball will be in the air.
- On both the out and in patterns, the players should be taught to keep running so the QB can properly time the pass.

Very seldom during a game do you have the opportunity to throw deep to one of your running backs. When you do, it may result in a very long gain or a touchdown, so it is important to teach two deep pass routes to your running backs. Speed is especially important for these two pass routes to give the quarterback enough time to throw the pass. In a game, the running back must realize the ball will be in the air for a longer period of time, and there is every possibility that he may have to adjust his path or stop and come back to make the catch.

The two deep pass routes are *fan* and *post*.

🏈 DEEP PASS ROUTES

Number of players: All RBs
Equipment: Shorts or full pads, markers
Time: 2 minutes/once a week

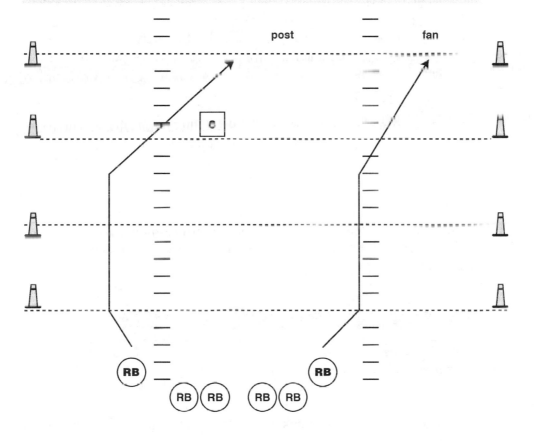

1. The first player in each group lines up in his RB stance and listens for the coach to call out the pass route (post or fan).
2. On the command of "Hut," both receivers run the pattern called (see below).
3. The players running the pattern go to the back of the line, and the next two RBs step up and get into their stance.
4. Each RB runs each pattern to both sides of the field.

Coaching Points

- In the beginning of the season, the players may need to go one at a time.
- Post Route:
  1. The RB starts to the line of scrimmage at a 45-degree angle outside his offensive tackle.
  2. He turns up the field the instant he reaches the line of scrimmage.

3. He drives up the field for 8 yards, then pivots on his inside foot, and runs at a deep angle to the center of the field toward the goal post.

4. In a game, he needs to look back over his inside shoulder and expect to run under the ball.

- Fan Route:
    1. The RB starts to the line of scrimmage at a 45-degree angle outside of his offensive tackle.
    2. He turns up the field the instant he reaches the line of scrimmage, pivots on his outside foot at 8 yards, and breaks at a deep angle to the sideline.
    3. He turns his head back to the QB by looking over his outside shoulder.
    4. In a game, the ball could be thrown to his outside, so he may have to come back to make the catch.

Blocking on Pass Plays

Many times when a team is throwing the ball, the running backs will need to block to protect the quarterback. Usually their block will be on a linebacker rushing from the outside of the offensive tackle or on a linebacker rushing inside the offensive tackle's block.

The running back's goal is to position his body between the rushing linebacker and the quarterback. He will not be able to attack the defensive man as he did on a running play. He waits for the rush man to come to him before making his block, and he stays with his block until the quarterback has had time to throw the ball.

BLOCKING AN OUTSIDE PASS RUSH

Number of players: All RBs
Equipment: Shorts or full pads, markers
Time: 3 minutes/once a week

1. The coach uses a chalk mark or shirt to mark the spot where the QB will set up to pass.
2. The coach designates which RB and outside rusher (OR) will execute drill.
3. Prior to starting the drill, each RB turns back to look at the spot where the QB will be.
4. The coach calls out "Down" to tell the RB to get into his stance.
5. On the command of "Hut," the RB sets up correctly as the OR starts across the line of scrimmage.
6. The RB stays in front of the OR until the coach calls out "Stop."
7. The RB goes to the end of the line, and the OR becomes the RB.
8. The running backs work from both sides of the field.

Coaching Points

- When first teaching pass protection blocking, have the OR rush at half speed.

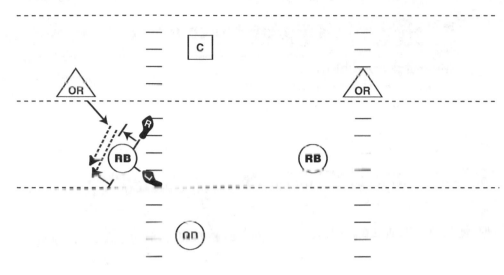

- Blocking Outside Pass Rush:
  1. On the command of "Hut," the RD steps up and in with his inside foot, then back with his outside foot.
  2. The OR rushes straight at the target area where the QB sets up to throw. (Instruct the ORs to not turn and face the RB making the block.)
  3. The RB faces out to the sideline. (By facing out to the sideline, the RB gives the OR only one way to go—up the field.)
  4. The RB's feet are parallel and slightly wider than shoulder-width apart.
  5. In this position, his knees are bent, his back straight, his head up, and his eyes focused straight ahead.
  6. His elbows are in close to his waist, and both hands are chest high with the palms facing forward and fingers spread.
  7. As the OR nears the RB, the RB slows his rush by striking the rusher in the center of his chest with the palm of the hand away from the line of scrimmage.
  8. He uses the palm of his other hand to strike the shoulder pad area of the rusher.
  9. Keeping his hips over his feet, the RB uses a shuffling motion (never crossing his feet) to drive the OR up the field past the spot where the QB will set up.

Blocking an inside rusher (IR) starts the same way with a good inside and forward step with the running back's inside foot. He then steps up with his outside foot, evens his stance, and looks directly upfield. A line drawn through his shoulders would be parallel with the line of scrimmage.

Running backs should move to a position where they are inside of the rusher so they can block the rusher to the outside and direct him past the quarterback.

🏈 BLOCKING AN INSIDE PASS RUSH

Number of players: All RBs
Equipment: Shorts or full pads, markers
Time: 3 minutes/once a week

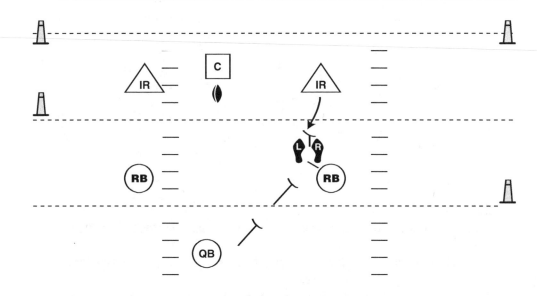

1. Using a chalk mark or shirt, the coach marks the spot where the QB will set up to pass.
2. The coach designates which RB and rush man will perform the drill.
3. Each RB turns back to see the spot where the QB will be.
4. The IR is instructed to try to rush through the RB to the QB spot.
5. The coach calls out "Down" to get the RB into his stance.
7. On the command of "Hut," the RB sets up correctly as the rusher starts across the line of scrimmage.
8. The RB stays in front of the IR until the coach calls out "Stop."
9. The RB goes to the end of the line, and the IR is now the RB.
10. Make certain the RBs work from both sides of the ball.

Coaching Points

- When first teaching pass protection blocking, have the IR rush at half speed.
- Blocking Inside Pass Rush:
    1. On the command of "Hut," the RB steps up and in with his inside foot.
    2. The RB's second step is up with his outside foot, so that he evens his stance and looks directly upfield. In this position, his body should be even with the line of scrimmage.
    3. As the IR rushes straight at the target area where the QB will set up to throw, the RB focuses his eyes on the IR's chest.

4. When the DR is close to the RB, the RB bends his knees and strikes the rusher in the chest with the palms of both hands, stopping the forward movement of the rusher.

5. When the RB makes contact with his hands, he extends his arms, creating space between himself and the rush man.

6. When the RB has moved away from the DR, coach him to shuffle his feet so that he is slightly inside of the DR.

• The RB should always maintain a position where he is between the rusher and the area where the QB will set up to throw.

The most difficult pass block for running backs is when an inside pass rusher is determined to rush inside the running back as he makes his pass block. The running back must be sure the defensive man is really rushing to his inside and not faking him so that he can quickly rush to the outside.

When the running back sees the defender's chest cross his nose, he can be fairly sure that the rusher is trying to rush up the middle and not to the outside.

🏈 BLOCKING AN UP-THE-MIDDLE PASS RUSH

Number of players: All RBs
Equipment: Shorts or full pads, markers
Time: 3 minutes/once a week

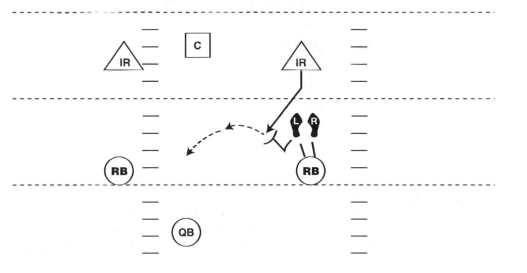

1. Using a chalk mark or shirt, the coach marks the spot where the QB will set up to pass.

2. The coach designates which RB and IR will perform the drill.

3. Each RB turns back to look at the spot where the QB will be.

4. The coach calls out "Down" to get the RB into his stance.
5. On the command of "Hut," the RB sets up correctly as the IR starts across the line of scrimmage.
6. The IR rushes directly at the RB and then veers to the inside to the OB spot.
7. The RB attempts to stay in front of the IR until the coach calls out "Stop."
8. The RB goes to the end of the line, and the IR is now the RB.
9. Make certain the RBs work from both sides of the ball.

Coaching Points

- When first teaching pass protection blocking, have the IR rush at half speed.
- Blocking Up-the-Middle Pass Rush:
  1. The RB sets up exactly as he does to block an inside pass rusher.
  2. The RB focuses on the IR's chest so he can quickly determine when the rusher's body is moving to the inside.
  3. When the RB sees the rusher moving in this direction, he steps back slightly with his inside foot and pushes off his inside leg.
  4. The RB hits the rusher in the chest with the palm of his inside hand to stop the IR's forward movement.
  5. As the RB makes contact with the inside hand, he quickly steps toward the IR with his outside foot.
  6. With this second step, he should be in position to hit out with the palm of his other hand and drive the rusher across the field to the other side of the ball.

Special Plays from Good Pass Blocking

A running back who is a good pass protection blocker helps your passing game and also helps on plays where the running back sets up to pass block and ends up with the ball.

Two plays you may want to teach to running backs, and include in your offense, are the *draw play* and the *screen pass*. On the draw play, the quarterback hands the ball to the running back as he drops to set up to pass. On a screen pass, the running back is a receiver and catches the ball after setting up to block.

For both plays, the running back sets up as he would to block an inside pass rusher. The offensive line sets up to pass block, and the quarterback drops back in the same way that he would if he were going to throw a pass.

Both of these plays (the draw and the screen) help your offense when you meet a defensive team that is good at rushing the passer. Both plays, when run successfully, have the effect of slowing down the defensive men as they pass rush and can keep linebackers from dropping off the line into zone coverage.

DRAW PLAY

Number of players: All RBs
Equipment: Shorts or full pads, markers, ball
Time: 2 minutes/once a week

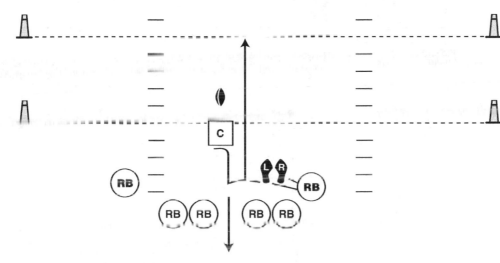

1. Two RBs line up in a split formation.
2. The coach lines up as a QB in his pre-snap position with the ball.
3. The coach designates which RB is to receive the handoff by calling out "Draw right or left."
4. On the command of "Hut," the RBs set up as if they were going to pass block.
5. The coach starts his drop, then hands the ball to the RB designated to run the draw.
6. The RB secures the ball and heads up the field running hard for 10 yards.
7. After 10 yards, he turns back and returns the ball to the coach.
8. The RB goes to the end of the line, and another RB takes his place in the formation.
9. The play is then run by the RB on the other side of the formation.
10. Make certain the RBs work from both sides of the ball.

Coaching Points

- Draw Play:
  1. On "Hut" the RB steps inside as if to block a defensive rusher.
  2. The RB steps laterally to the inside with his inside foot and brings his outside foot to the inside so he has a balanced stance.
  3. He bends his knees and keeps his back straight. His head is up, and his eyes are focused on the offensive line.

4. The RB positions his arms just as he would to take a handoff, with the inside arm on top and the outside hand forming the bottom of the pocket.
5. He waits in position and allows the QB to place the ball in the pocket.
6. Once the ball is secure, the RB immediately starts up the field running hard for 10 yards.

🏈 SCREEN PASS

Number of players: All RBs
Equipment: Shorts or full pads, markers, ball
Time: 2 minutes/once a week

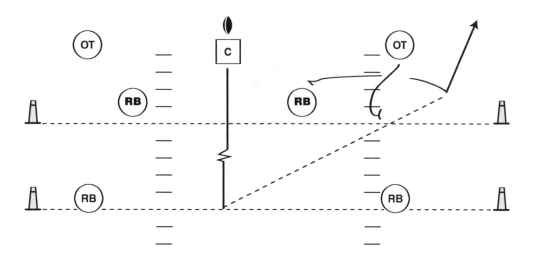

1. Two RBs line up in a split formation.
2. The coach lines up as QB in his pre-snap position with the ball.
3. The next two RBs line up as OTs.
4. The coach designates which RB receives the pass by calling out "Screen right or left."
5. On the command of "Hut," the RBs set up as if they were going to pass block, and the two OTs drop back 4 yards as if they were executing a pass protection block.
6. The coach starts his drop, hesitates at 7 yards to time the screen, then drops to 11 yards to throw the ball to the screen back.
7. The RB makes the catch, secures the ball, and heads up the field running hard for 10 yards.
8. After 10 yards, he turns back and returns the ball to the coach.
9. The RB goes to the end of the line, another RB becomes the OT, and the OT moves into the backfield position.
10. The play is then run by the RB on the other side of the formation.
11. Make certain that the RBs work from both sides of the field.

Coaching Points

- Screen Pass:
  1. On "Hut" the RB must step inside as if he is going to block a pass rusher.
  2. He looks upfield and stays alert for any blitzing linebacker. (In a game the RB would stop up and deliver a hit on the linebacker, momentarily stopping his rush to the QB.)
  3. The RB counts out loud to a thousand-three as he stays in his pass blocking position.
  4. After counting to a thousand-three, he moves forward for two steps toward the line of scrimmage.
  5. Once the OT has passed his position, the RB moves to the outside of the formation.
  6. The RB immediately turns his head back over his outside shoulder to the QB (screen right would be his right shoulder). The pass should arrive over this shoulder.
  7. Have him concentrate on making the catch and securing the ball.
  8. Have him yell "go" to alert his offensive blockers that he has the ball.
  9. He then turns up the field, running hard for 10 yards.

Quarterback Drills

This chapter focuses on basic drills for the quarterback. Many of the drills you will use during this period are *combination drills*, where the quarterbacks coordinate with another group of offensive players. During these drills, you may need to introduce the ball into the drill.

The following drills will be run mainly by the coach and quarterbacks with the occasional addition of a running back for the handoff drill.

2-POINT STANCE

Number of players: All QBs
Equipment: Shorts or full pads
Time: 2 minutes/every day

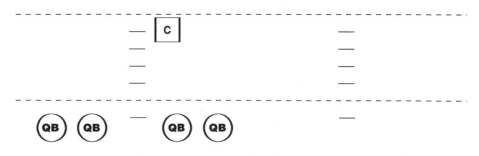

1. All QBs line up across the field facing the coach.
2. On the command of "Stance," each player gets into his proper stance (see below).
3. The coach scans the line to see that everyone is properly set.
4. On the coach's command of "Up," players come out of their stances to an upright position.

Quarterback in a 2-point stance. (left)

Side view of quarterback in a 2-point stance. (right)

Coaching Points

- In the beginning of the year, go one player at a time until you are confident that each player understands his stance.
- 2-Point Stance:
  1. The QB starts by bending his knees to lower his upper body, while keeping his feet pointing straight ahead.
  2. With his knees flexed, he bends forward at the hips, bringing his shoulders and head in front of his hips.
  3. His back is straight, shoulders even, head up, and eyes focused straight ahead.
  4. From this position, the QB extends both arms in front of his hips, bringing both hands together. His passing hand is on top and the heels of both hands are together.
  5. He reaches forward with both hands, keeping his thumbs together but with his fingers extended and separated.

 **START**

Number of players:	All QBs
Equipment:	Shorts or full pads
Time:	2 minutes/every day

1. All QBs line up across the field facing the coach.
2. Then the coach gives the command "Stance."
3. The coach calls out the direction that he wants the players to start: right and left, angle right and left, sweep right and left, or pitch right and left.

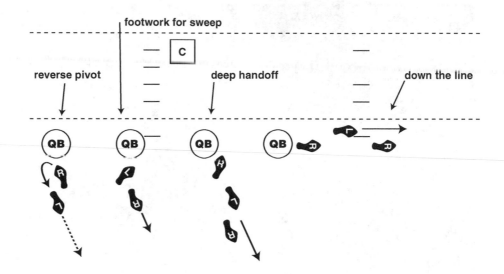

4. On the command of "Hut," each player starts properly and moves three or four steps in the correct direction (see below).

5. After making their start, the players line up again and repeat the drill.

Coaching Points

- Check that each QB is in a proper stance.

- For plays in which a QB is moving down the line of scrimmage to his right or left, the QB takes a very short directional "cheat" step with the foot on the side you have called out. This should turn his head, eyes, hips, and body to the sideline. His second step is longer, and he extends the hand closest to the line, as he will when making the handoff. He will use this start if you run a *down the line* option play, only now when he comes down the line, he can either toss the ball back with the hand away from the line or turn up the field and run.

- Next have the QB move away from the line at an angle as he would to make a handoff deeper in the backfield. Now he must start with a short step back with the foot on the side of the handoff. His second, longer step with the opposite foot should carry him at an angle away from his snap position. Next he extends the hand nearest the line for the handoff.

- When working on the footwork for a sweep to either side of the ball, the QB begins with a step back with the foot opposite from the RB's direction (sweep right = left foot). Make certain that the second, longer step moves him back away from the line, putting him in position to make the handoff. He now extends the hand on the side of his turn for the handoff, ending up with his body turned away from the line of scrimmage.

- Finally, have QBs work on using a reverse pivot motion, which is needed to hand off the ball in close or to pitch the ball wide. The QB starts with a short step, using the foot that is on the side of the play. He pivots around on this foot with his second step. When he is in his actual pivot, he will have his back to the line of scrimmage for an instant. For the handoff, he extends the hand closest to the line of scrimmage. When pitching the ball, make certain that he has the ball in both hands, keeps his hands on his hip as he turns, then extends both hands as if to pitch the ball underhanded to the back.

- In the beginning of the year, go one player at a time until you are confident that each player understands how to start correctly.

Quarterback Pass Drop Drills

It is essential for the quarterback to learn the proper footwork for the different types of movements he will need when passing the ball. These drills should be done without throwing the ball. The first will be a 3-Step Drop that should be used for all short passes to the tight end or wide receivers.

3-STEP DROP

Number of players: All QBs
Equipment: Shorts or full pads, markers
Time: 2 minutes/every day

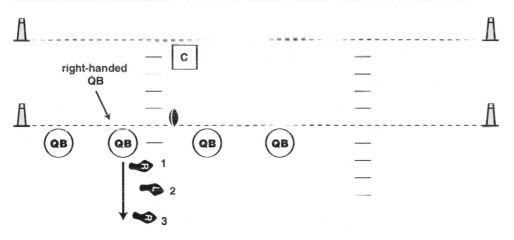

1. All QBs line up across the field facing the coach and assume the proper stance upon command by the coach.
2. Then the coach calls out "3-step drop."
3. On the command of "Hut," each player takes a 3-step drop and sets up to throw (see below).
4. After making their drop, the players line up again and repeat the drill.

Coaching Points

- 3-Step Drop:
    1. Check that each QB is in a proper stance.
    2. On the command of "Hut," each QB takes a short step forward with the foot opposite his passing hand (do not count this step).
    3. The QB's first real step is away from the line of scrimmage with the foot on the side of his passing hand.

4. For the second step, he takes a crossover step with his other foot.
5. Finally, with the foot on the side of the passing hand, he takes the third step that stops his momentum away from the line.
6. He then brings both feet under his hips and stands tall with both hands held chest high.
- In the beginning of the year, go through the drill one player at a time until you're confident that each player understands how to drop correctly.

Once the quarterbacks have mastered the 3-step drop, you can begin to have them drill on a *5-step drop* to get into proper position to throw medium and deep pass routes to all receivers.

5-STEP DROP

Number of players: All QBs
Equipment: Shorts or full pads
Time: 2 minutes/every day

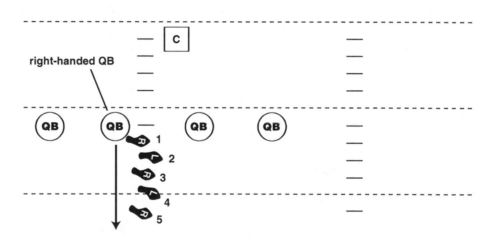

1. All of the QBs line up across the field facing the coach and assume the proper stance upon command by the coach.
2. The coach should then call out "5-step drop" (see below).
3. On the command of "Hut," each player starts properly, takes a 5-step drop, and sets up to throw.
4. After making their drop, players line up again and repeat the drill.

Coaching Points
- 5-Step Drop:
  1. On the command of "Hut," each QB takes a short step forward with the foot opposite his passing hand. (This short step is not counted as one of the five.)

2. The QB's first real step is away from the line of scrimmage with the foot on the side of his passing hand.

3. For the second step, he takes a crossover step with his other foot.

4. The third step is a crossover step with the foot on the side of the passing hand (third step).

5. The fourth step is another crossover step with his other foot.

6. Finally he takes a final, somewhat elongated, crossover step that stops his momentum away from the line.

7. He then brings both feet under his hips and stands tall with both hands held chest high.

- In the beginning of the year, go one player at a time until you are confident that each player understands how to drop correctly.

Quarterback sets up to throw.

MOVEMENT PASSING

Number of players: All QBs
Equipment: Shorts or full pads, markers
Time: 2 minutes/every day

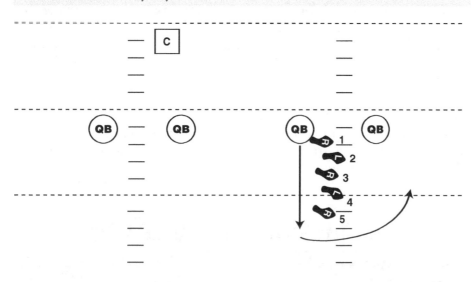

1. All of the QBs line up across the field facing the coach and assume the proper stance upon command by the coach.
2. The coach calls out right or left, indicating which direction the QBs are to move to make the throw.
3. On the command of "Hut," each QB takes a 5-step drop, then turns and moves to the proper side to set up a throw.
4. After making their directional move, the QBs line up again and repeat the drill.

Coaching Points

- Movement Passing:
  1. Make certain that each QB takes the correct 5-step drop before moving to the outside to throw.
  2. At the end of his 5-step drop, the QB turns his body to the sideline and sprints in that direction.
  3. As he moves to the outside and prepares to throw, the first thing the QB must do is get his hips turned down the field, pointing directly at the target.
  4. To begin his throwing motion, he moves his body in the direction of the pass by stepping with the foot opposite his throwing arm.
  5. Make certain that this lead step is directed at his target.
  6. When the QB is moving to the same side as his passing arm, getting turned will be much easier.
  7. When the QB moves to the side opposite his throwing arm, he should go a little deeper in the backfield to give himself room to get turned upfield.
  8. As the QB's hips and opposite foot lead the throw, his passing arm is then in position to move forward in a normal, high throwing motion.
  9. It is important for him to keep moving forward through the entire throwing motion and keep his momentum moving at the target, releasing the ball as his body moves over the lead foot.
  10. Finally, he finishes with a continuing step with the foot on the same side as his passing arm.
- In the beginning of the year, go one player at a time until you're confident that each player understands how to drop correctly.

Taking the Snap

Each offensive play will begin with the center snapping the ball to the quarterback. Emphasize to your quarterbacks that taking the snap and securing the ball are essential for offensive success.

TAKING THE SNAP AND PROPER GRIP

Number of players: All QBs
Equipment: Shorts or full pads, ball
Time: 2 minutes/every day

1. All QBs line up across the field facing the coach, who is on one knee with the ball.
2. One at a time, each QB takes his stance in front of the ball.
3. The coach then raises the ball up to the QB's hands.
4. The coach checks the player's grip on the ball.
5. After the coach sees the QB has the ball in his grasp, the QB gives the ball to the coach and goes to the end of the line.

Coaching Points

- Once the players are doing the drill correctly, have them pair up and lift the ball to one another.
- Check that each QB is in a proper stance and his hands are in the correct position to accept the ball.
- As you bring the ball up sideways to his hands, check that he quickly closes around the ball with both hands.
- He should grip the ball with both hands and immediately cradle it in the pocket.
- Check his grip to make sure he has the correct hand position on the ball:
  - Passing hand covers the laces and is near the center of the ball.
  - Little finger is on the laces; second and third fingers extend over the laces.
  - Index finger is across the seam, not on the laces, and close to the point of the ball.
  - Thumb on his passing hand is on the next panel.
  - Fingers are spread, and he has control of the ball.
- The other hand should grip the ball from the other side.
- Once the player learns to take the snap and grip the ball correctly, you can tell him to move right or left or to drop back with the ball.

Quarterback demonstrates proper grip on the ball. Third finger could also be over the laces.

Making and Faking a Handoff

🏈 MAKING THE HANDOFF

Number of players: All QBs and an RB
Equipment: Shorts or full pads, ball
Time: 4 minutes/once a week

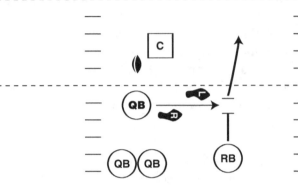

Quarterback sets up for a handoff. If this photo were taken from the running back's position, the quarterback should be preparing to hand off with his right hand, not his left.

1. Prior to the start of the drill, one QB lines up in position to take the snap and another QB is in position as the RB.
2. The coach lines up on one knee with the ball and makes the snap.
3. The coach designates what movement the QB is to take to make the handoff (e.g., dive right or left, sweep right or left) and positions the RB accordingly.
4. On the QB's command of "Hut," the coach hands him the ball to start the drill.
5. Once the QB takes the snap and simulates the handoff, he rotates to the end of the line, and the RB takes the QB's position and hands the ball to the coach.

Coaching Points

- Repeat the drill so every player has an opportunity to make the handoff going to their right and left.
- Check that the QB is in a proper stance, his hands are in the correct position to accept the ball, and he takes the snap correctly.
- Make certain he uses the correct footwork to make the handoff and that he is looking at the RB as he starts his move.
- Check that the QB places the ball firmly in the RB's pocket, with his hand nearest the line of scrimmage.

- After making the handoff, the QB drops back as if to pass.
- Emphasize that it is the QB's responsibility to get the ball into the RB's pocket.

After the quarterbacks are successfully making the handoff and placing the ball in the running back's pocket without a fumble, you can teach them how to fake the handoff, keep the ball, and either drop back or move to the outside to get in position to pass the ball.

Quarterback places the ball into the running back's pocket. The running back secures the ball.

 **FAKING THE HANDOFF**

Number of players: All QBs and an RB
Equipment: Shorts or full pads, ball
Time: 4 minutes/once a week

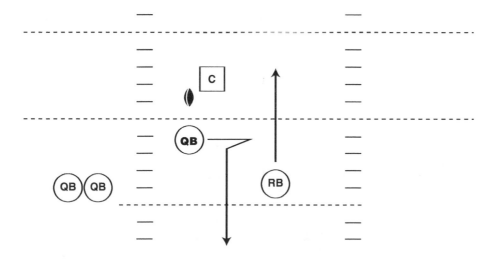

1. Prior to the start of the drill, one QB lines up in position to take the snap and another QB is in position as the RB.
2. The coach lines up on one knee with the ball and makes the snap.
3. The coach designates what movement the QB is to take to fake the handoff (e.g., dive right or left, sweep right or left).

4. On the QB's command of "Hut," the coach hands him the ball to start the drill.

5. Once the QB takes the snap, fakes the handoff, and sets up to pass, he rotates to the end of the line, and the RB takes the QB's position and hands the ball to the coach.

Coaching Points

- Repeat the drill so every player has an opportunity to fake the handoff and set up to pass moving to both his right and left.
- Check that the QB is in a proper stance, his hands are in the correct position to accept the ball, and he takes the snap correctly.
- Make certain the QB uses the correct footwork to make his move to the RB, and that he is looking at the RB as he starts his motion.
- Check that the QB places the ball firmly on his hip with the hand away from the line of scrimmage.
- As he reaches the RB, the QB extends the hand closest to the line of scrimmage, places that hand into the RB's pocket, then quickly brings it back to his own body.
- After faking the handoff, the QB takes a 5-step drop from the line and sets up to pass, bringing the ball up to his chest and securing it with both hands.
- Emphasize that it is the QB's responsibility to make a good fake with the empty hand into the RB's pocket.

Basic Skills and Drills

Two basic skills must be taught to every player on your team—tackling and catching. Obviously defensive players perform some form of tackling every practice. For the offensive players and special team specialists, tackling skills may only be used once or twice a week at the most.

Tackling

With very young players, you need to take into consideration that many of your players may be coming to the field with a very natural fear of contact and especially of tackling. They may not verbalize this fear to you or their teammates, but you should introduce tackling on a gradual basis under a very controlled type of drill. This means matching up players of the same size and temperament whenever possible. Start your teaching by having the players go at half speed in the drill until you feel comfortable that they can execute the tackle in the safest manner.

As the coach, be sure to emphasize the importance that all players know how to tackle properly. Defensive players have the opportunity to tackle on every play. Offensive players may have to go on defense and must be able to tackle anytime there is a fumble recovery or an interception. Tackling becomes extremely important for a special teams player on any of the coverage teams., Every player may be put in the situation of having to make a tackle at some point during the game and season.

Helmet Safety

Continually emphasize to the players that they must use their shoulder pads to make a tackle—NEVER their helmet. Their helmet is for protection; it is not to be used for blocking or tackling.

STRAIGHT-ON TACKLING

Number of players: All defense
Equipment: Full pads, markers
Time: 4 minutes/every practice

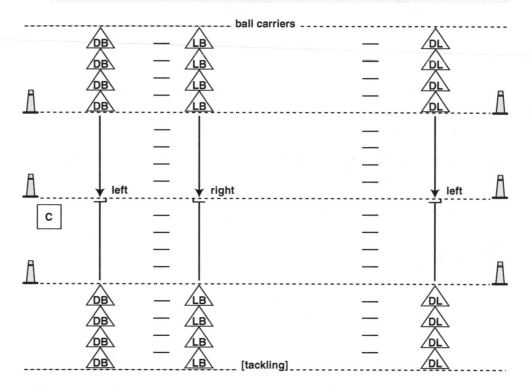

1. Players line up 10 yards apart and face one another.
2. The coach designates which side is tackling and which shoulder they should use to make the tackle (left or right).
3. On the command of "Hut," the tacklers and the ball carriers advance toward one another at half speed.
4. The player acting as the ball carrier runs at half speed straight at the tackler and jumps up into the air as the tackle is made (see below).
5. Once the tackle is made, the tackler goes to the end of the ball carrier line, and the ball carrier goes to the end of the line of tacklers.

Coaching Points

- You may want to go one line at a time when first teaching the drill.
- The speed of the drill may be increased once the players are tackling correctly.
- Straight-on Tackling
    1. As the tackler nears the ball carrier, the tackler shortens his stride, widens his base, and lowers his hips by bending his knees.

2. At the same time, he keeps his back straight, his head up, and his eyes open and focused on the center of the ball carrier's chest.

3. The tackler needs to explode off the foot on the side of the shoulder that he is using to make the tackle.

4. He makes contact with the designated shoulder pad and his head slides to the side.

5. On contact, the tackler drives his shoulder up and through the ball carrier's chest, wraps both arms around the ball carrier's body and grabs the ball carrier's jersey in both hands.

6. He continues his leg drive and attempts to lift and carry the ball carrier back a few steps.

7. In a game, the tackler would take the ball carrier to the ground.

You can also use this drill to teach your offensive and special teams players to tackle correctly, again matching them by position as they learn.

All Players Need to Practice Tackling

Many times during a game, a player needs to tackle a ball carrier who is angling away from him and not coming at him straight on. This type of tackling can be taught with the following drill.

A straight-on tackle.

🏈 TACKLING ON AN ANGLE

Number of players: All defense
Equipment: Full pads, markers
Time: 4 minutes/every practice

1. Players line up by position in two groups, facing each other and 13 to 15 yards apart.

2. The coach designates which side is tackling and which direction the BC should cut at 5 yards (left or right).

3. On the command of "Hut," the tacklers and ball carriers advance toward one another for 5 yards at half speed.

4. At 5 yards, each ball carrier angles in the designated direction.

5. Then each tackler changes his path to meet the ball carrier.

6. The ball carrier runs at half speed and leans into the tackler as the tackle is being made (see below).

7. Once the tackle is made, the tackler goes to the end of the ball carrier line, and the ball carrier goes to the end of the tackler line.

Coaching Points

- You may only want to go one line at a time when first teaching this drill.
- Increase the speed of the drill once the players are tackling correctly.

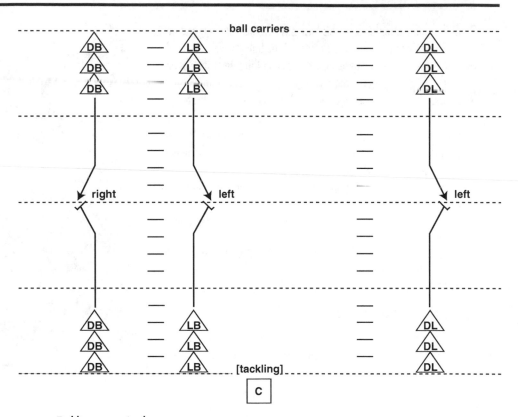

- Tackling on an Angle:
  1. As the tackler nears the ball carrier, he shortens his stride, widens his base, and lowers his hips by bending his knees.
  2. At the same time, he keeps his back straight, his head up, and his eyes open and focused on the center of the ball carrier's chest.
  3. The tackler needs to explode off the foot nearest the ball carrier and use the shoulder on that same side to make contact with the ball carrier (i.e., a tackler angling to his right hits with his left shoulder).
  4. He makes contact with the designated shoulder pad and his head slides to the front of the ball carrier.
  5. On contact, the tackler drives his shoulder up and through the ball carrier's chest, wrapping both arms around the ball carrier's body and grabbing the ball carrier's jersey in both hands.
  6. He continues his leg drive and attempts to lift and carry the ball carrier back a few steps.
  7. In a game, the tackler would take the ball carrier to the ground.

You can also use this drill to teach your offensive and special teams players to tackle correctly, again matching them by position as they learn.

Catching

How to properly catch the ball is the second basic skill every player needs to know. Again emphasize how important it is for all players to know how to catch properly. Offensive receivers, tight ends, and running backs have the most opportunity to catch the ball. Defensive players may have the chance to make a big play when they make an interception. Receiving skills can come into play on special teams when you decide to fake a kick and throw the ball instead. As with tackling, sometime during the season, every player may be put in the situation of having to make a reception in the game when a ball is tipped or bounces off a receiver's hands. Even the quarterback may get a chance to make a catch on a pass from a running back or on a pass that is deflected high into the air.

When teaching young players to catch, focus on these three major points:

1. Hand position
2. Arm extension
3. Ball concentration

🏈 HAND POSITION

Number of players: all WRs, TEs, RBs
Equipment: Shorts or full pads
Time: 4 minutes/once a week

(WR) (WR) (WR) (TE) (TE) (RB) (RB) (RB) (RB) (RB) (RB) (TE) (TE) (WR) (WR) (WR)

C

1. Players line up in one line across the field facing the coach. If there are too many, have them line up one group at a time.
2. The players get in a comfortable 2-point stance with their feet even and spread the width of their hips.
3. The coach calls out one of nine directions: low (right, center, or left), chest (right, center, or left), and high (right, center, or left).
4. On the command of "Hut," each player reaches to the designated direction and forms his hands in the proper position (see below). He holds his hands in this spot until the coach calls "Up."

Correct hand position to receive a low pass. (left)

Correct hand position to receive a high pass. (right)

5. The coach calls out another spot and quickly repeats the drill.

Coaching Points

- For any reception in the low area, make certain that the players have their little fingers together, with their fingers spread and their palms up.
- For any pass at the chest level or higher, check that the players have their thumbs together, their fingers spread, and their wrists cocked back so their palms are pointing slightly up.
- Make certain that each player extends his arms away from his body as he positions his hands, and that his eyes are focused on the ball.

HEAD-ON CATCHING

Number of players: All WRs, TEs, RBs
Equipment: Shorts or full pads, 2 balls
Time: 4 minutes/once a week

1. Players line up by position in four lines across the field and face the coach.
2. The players get in a comfortable 2-point stance with their feet even and spread the width of their hips.
3. The coach designates which receiver is going to make the catch.
4. The coach throws the ball in one of the nine directions: low (right,

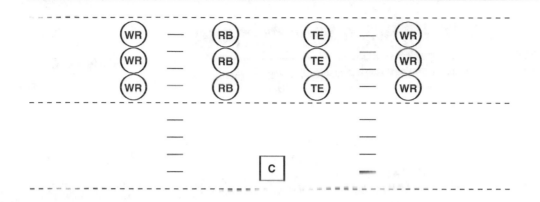

center, or left), chest (right, center, or left), and high (right, center, or left).

5. As the ball arrives, each player reaches out for the ball and forms his hands in the proper position to make the catch (see below).
6. After making the reception and securing the ball, the player runs the ball back to the coach.
7. The coach points out the next receiver and quickly repeats the drill.

Coaching Points

- Have each group of players line up on both your right and left on different days.
- For any reception in the low area, make certain that the players have their little fingers together, with their fingers spread and their palms up.
- For any pass at the chest level or higher, check that the players have their thumbs together, their fingers spread, and their wrists cocked back so their palms are pointing up.
- Make certain that each player extends his arms away from his body as he positions his hands, and that his eyes are focused on the ball.
- Emphasize that the player should look at his hands and the ball at the moment of the catch.
- Coach the player to immediately secure the ball against his side as he makes the reception and to return the ball to you.

Correct hand position to receive an outside or inside pass.

🏈 OUTSIDE/INSIDE CATCHING

Number of players: All WRs, TEs, and RBs
Equipment: Full pads or shorts, 2 balls
Time: 4 minutes/once a week

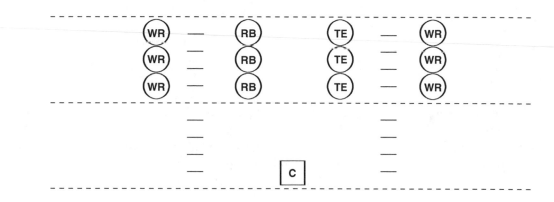

1. Players line up by position in four lines across the field, 6 yards away, and face the coach.
2. The players get in a comfortable 2-point stance with their feet even and spread the width of their hips.
3. Each group of players turns so they are facing the sideline on their side of the field for an outside reception and to the center of the field for an inside reception.
4. The coach designates which receiver will make the catch. The other players stand back far enough so that he can take a few steps when making the catch.
5. The designated player runs in place, then moves forward as much as possible to make the catch.
6. The coach throws the ball in front of the receivers in one of the three directions: low, chest high, and high above their shoulder pads.
7. As the ball arrives, each player reaches out for the ball, forming their hands in the proper position to make the catch (see below).
8. After making the reception, the player runs the ball back to the coach and hands him the ball after he's made the next throw.
9. The coach points out the next receiver and quickly repeats the drill.

Coaching Points

- Have each group of players line up on both your right and left on different days.

- For any reception in the low area, make certain that the players have their little fingers together, with their fingers spread and their palms up.
- For any pass at the chest level or higher, check that the players have their thumbs together, their fingers spread and their wrists cocked back so their palms are pointing up.
- Make certain that each player extends his arms away from his body as he positions his hands, and that his eyes are focused on the ball.
- Emphasize that the player should see his hands and the ball at the moment of the catch.
- For an outside reception, the player turns his head and shoulders back to the ball and reaches back with his hands and arms.
- On an inside pass, he should be looking right at you and reaching forward for the ball.
- Coach the player to immediately secure the ball against his side as he makes the reception and to return the ball to you.

Correct hand position to receive an over-the-shoulder pass.

🏈 OVER-THE-SHOULDER CATCHING

Number of players: All WRs, TEs, RBs
Equipment: Shorts or full pads, markers, 2 balls
Time: 4 minutes/once a week

1. Players line up by position in four lines across the field, 7 yards from the coach, with their backs to him and facing the goal line.
2. The players get in a comfortable 2-point stance with their feet even and spread the width of their hips.
3. Each group of players turns so they are looking up the field.
4. The coach designates which receiver will make the catch.
5. The designated player runs in place until the coach calls "Hut," then he moves forward to make the catch.
6. The coach throws the ball in front of the receivers in one of the two directions: over the inside or outside shoulder.
7. As the ball arrives, each player reaches out for the ball, forming their hands in the proper position to make the catch (see below).
8. After making the reception and securing the ball, the player runs the ball back to the coach and hands him the ball after he has made the next throw.
9. The coach points out the next receiver and quickly repeats the drill.

Coaching Points

- Have each group of players line up on both your right and left on different days.

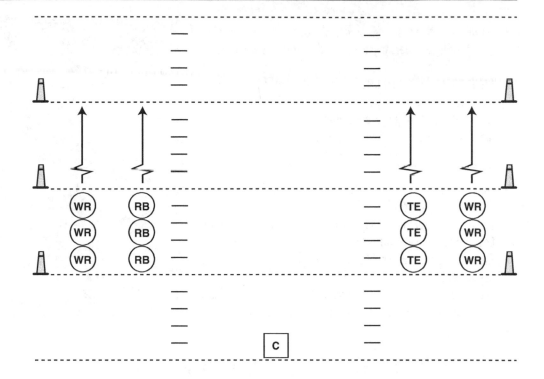

- For any reception in front of them and over either shoulder, make certain that the players have their little fingers together, their fingers spread, and their palms up.
- Make certain that each player extends his arms away from his body, reaching back as he positions his hands, with his eyes focused on the ball.
- Emphasize that the player should see his hands and the ball at the moment of the catch.
- For either reception, the receiver turns his head to the side of the ball's flight so he can follow the ball to his hands.
- Coach the player to immediately secure the ball against his side as he makes the reception and to return the ball to you.

You can also use these drills to teach your defensive and special teams players to catch correctly, again matching them by position as they learn.

Combination Drills for Individual Practice

During your individual period, and once the skills needed for each position have been mastered, it will often be good to combine segments of your offense or defense and special teams to let them have practice time together. Unless you are introducing new skills or materials, these drills should be run at full speed so each player gets a feeling for executing the skill at game speed.

Offensive Combination Drills

 ## BALL HANDLING

Number of players: all RBs and QBs, and CN
Equipment: Shorts or full pads, markers, ball
Time: 4 minutes/once a week

1. Prior to the start of the drill, a QB and two running backs line up in the correct formation for the play called.
3. On the command of "Hut," the CN snaps the ball and the QB and running backs run the play.
4. Once the QB makes the handoff, he carries out his assignment for a play action pass.
5. The running back who gets the handoff sprints downfield with the ball for at least 10 yards, then returns the ball to the CN.
6. The running backs rotate every play and the QB runs four plays, two to the right and two to the left, before changing positions.

Coaching Points

- It is good to have a CN in the drill, but if one is not available, the coach can line up on one knee with the ball and make the snap.

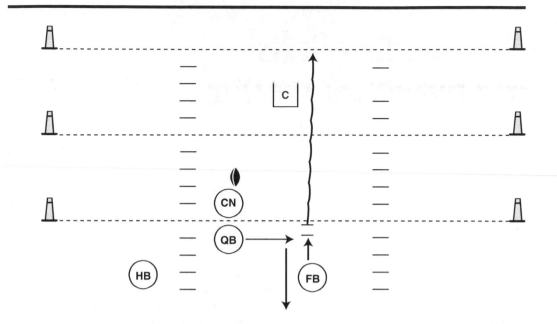

- Repeat the drill so every player has an opportunity to make the handoff going to his right and left.
- Check that the QB and running backs are lined up properly in the correct stance prior to the snap.
- Make certain they use the proper footwork to make the handoff to have a good mesh between the two:
  1. Check that the QB places the ball firmly in the running back's pocket using the hand nearest the line of scrimmage.
  2. Make certain that the RB grasps the ball and secures it right away.
- After making the handoff, the QB drops back as if to pass.
- Emphasize that it is the responsibility of the QB to get the ball into the running back's pocket and the running back's responsibility to secure the ball.

🏈 WR PASS RECEIVING

Number of players: All QBs and WRs, and CN
Equipment: Full pads, markers, ball
Time: 6 minutes/twice a week

1. Prior to the start of the drill, the QB and wide receivers line up in the proper position for the pass pattern called.
2. On the command of "Hut," the CN snaps the ball, and the QB and wide receivers make the correct movements for the pass route called.
3. The wide receiver who gets the pass sprints downfield with the ball for at least 10 yards, then returns the ball to the CN.

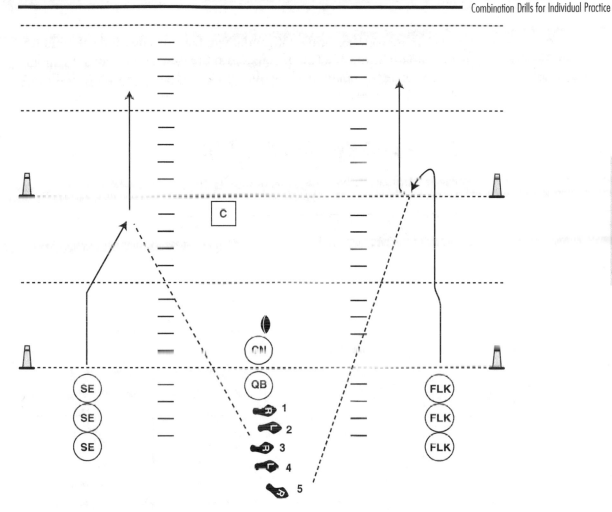

Coaching Points

- In the beginning, designate which WR is going to run the pass route. Later if you have two QBs, you can set them both up in the drill, run both wide receivers on the pass route called, and throw simultaneously to both sides of the field.
- Be sure to alternate sides for the wide receivers and the QBs if you are using two QBs in the drill.
- It's good to have a CN in the drill, but if one is not available, the coach can line up on one knee with the ball and make the snap.
- Make certain the receivers start correctly by taking a first step forward and drive up the field to the proper depth before running the pass route.
- Check that the QB drops correctly with 3 or 5 steps and steps at the target to make the throw.
- Make certain that the receiver has his hands in the proper position based on the location of the ball, that he's reaching out for the ball, and that he secures the ball immediately after the catch.

At another area of the field, you can run a similar passing drill at the same time for the tight ends and running backs. This, of course, will depend on the size of your coaching staff, and if you have two quarterbacks on the team who can throw the ball. If you do run the two drills at the same time, you can rotate the quarterbacks so they each have an opportunity to throw to both groups of receivers.

TE AND RB PASS RECEIVING

Number of players: QBs, TEs, RBs, and CN
Equipment: Full pads, markers, ball
Time: 6 minutes/twice a week

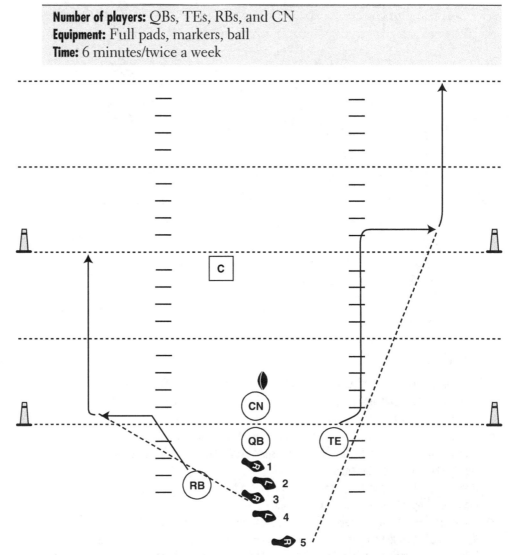

1. Prior to the start of the drill a QB, TE, and RB line up in their proper positions for the pass patterns called.
2. On the command of "Hut," the CN snaps the ball and the QB, TE, or RB make the correct movements for the pass route called.

3. The TE or RB who gets the pass sprints downfield with the ball for at least 10 yards, then returns the ball to the CN.

Coaching Points

- In the beginning of the season, designate which TE or RB is going to run the pass route. Later, if you have two QBs, and you are running only one drill at a time, you can set them both up in the drill, run both the TE and RB on a pass route, and throw simultaneously to both sides of the field.
- Be sure to alternate sides for the TE, RB, and the QBs.
- It is good to have a CN in the drill, but if one is not available, the coach can line up on one knee with the ball and make the snap.
- Make certain the receivers start correctly by taking a first step forward and drive up the field to the proper depth before running the pass route called.
- Check that the QB drops correctly with 3 or 5 steps and steps at the target to make the throw.
- Make certain that the receiver has his hands in the proper position based on the location of the ball, that he reaches out for the ball, and he secures the ball immediately after the catch.

Defensive Combination Drills

During this period, you have the opportunity to combine segments of your defense (line, linebackers, secondary) and work different areas of your defense without the need for offensive players. Working in this fashion, you have the ability to maintain individual coaching and at the same time begin to show the players how the three segments of the defense need to function as one unit.

This type of practice is especially beneficial if you have a limited coaching staff or when you first introduce a new defensive front maneuver or pass coverage. These types of drills also involve a number of players, so everyone stays active.

DROPPING INTO A 2-DEEP ZONE

Number of players: All LBs and DBs
Equipment: Shorts or full pads, markers, ball
Time: 5 minutes/once a week

1. Prior to the start of the drill, the linebackers and defensive backs line up in the proper position for the defense called.
2. On the command of "Hut," the QB drops back with the ball away from the line, and the linebackers and defensive backs drop into their zones.
3. The ball is then pointed into an area of the field, and all seven defensive players react in that direction (see below). The ball is not thrown.
4. A new group of seven players takes the field to repeat the drill.

Drop 2-Deep Zone

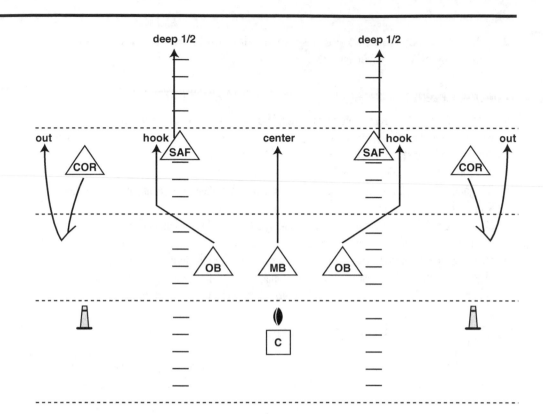

Coaching Points

- It is good to have a QB in the drill, but if one is not available, the coach can line up with the ball and serve as the QB.
- Make certain that all the players are using the correct technique to drop and move to their assigned zones.
- Dropping into a 2-Deep Zone:
    1. All players are looking back to the QB and the ball.
    2. When the QB sets up and is ready to throw, the players in the underneath zones stop getting depth and keep their feet moving in place.
    3. The two deep players keep getting depth until the QB actually starts his passing motion.
    4. All the players turn and sprint to the area where the QB points the ball.
    5. The two SAFs drop into the deep half of the field on their side, the two COs into the outside zone on their side, both OBs into the hook zone on their side, and the MB into the center zone.

DROPPING INTO A 3-DEEP ZONE

Number of players: All LBs and DBs
Equipment: Shorts or full pads, markers, ball
Time: 5 minutes/once a week

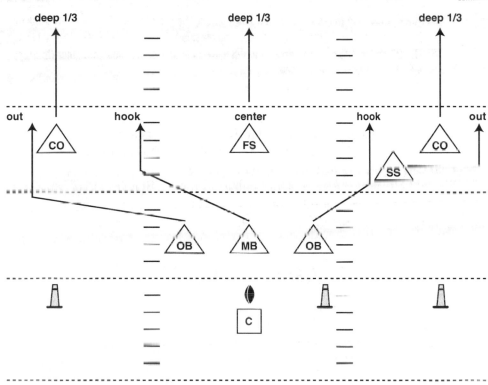

Drop 3-Deep Zone

1. Prior to the start of the drill, the linebackers and defensive backs line up in the proper position for the defense called.
2. It is good to have a QB in the drill, but if one is not available, the coach can line up with the ball and serve as the quarterback.
3. On the command of "Hut," the coach or QB drops back with the ball away from the line, and the linebackers and defensive backs drop into their correct zones.
4. The ball is then pointed into an area of the field, and all seven defensive players should react in that direction (see below). The ball is not thrown.
5. A new group of seven players takes the field to repeat the drill.

Coaching Points

- Make certain that all the players are using the correct technique to drop and move to their assigned zones.
- Dropping into a 3-Deep Zone:
  1. All players are looking back to the quarterback and the ball.
  2. When the quarterback sets up and is ready to throw, the players in the underneath zones stop getting depth and keep their feet moving in place.
  3. The three deep players keep getting depth until the quarterback actually starts his passing motion.
  4. All the players turn and sprint to the area where the quarterback points the ball.

5. The FS drops into the center deep third of the field, the two COs into the deep third zone on their side, and the SS into the outside zone on his side.
6. The OB on the side of the SS drops into the hook zone on his side, while the other OB drops into the outside zone on his side.
7. The MB drops into the hook zone opposite the SS.

You can also bring your defensive linemen together with your linebackers and run all of the blitzes you are planning to run in the game. The drill can be used to review all of your blitz packages, and you can be certain about the players' knowledge of their assignments. Because there is no contact, you can have a number of repetitions during each drill period. The following is an example of how you can set up this type of combination drill.

🏈 OUTSIDE LINEBACKER BLITZ

Number of players: All LBs and DLs
Equipment: Shorts or full pads, markers, ball
Time: 5 minutes/once a week

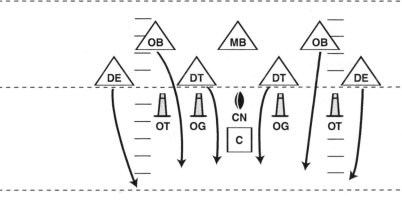

1. Prior to the start of the drill, the linebackers and defensive linemen line up in the proper positions for the defense called.
2. On the command of "Hut," the ball is snapped, and the defensive linemen and two OBs rush through their assigned gaps between the markers.
3. A new group of seven players takes the field to repeat the drill.

Coaching Points

- It is good to have a center and a quarterback in the drill, but if they are not available, the coach can line up, serve as the QB, and take the snap from a defensive player.
- Make certain that the defensive players are looking at the ball and begin their charge the instant the ball is snapped.

- Check that the two OBs are not leaning forward or moving prior to the snap.
- Outside Linebacker Blitz:
  1. The defensive linemen charge hard and low across the line through their designated gaps.
  2. The two DEs rush just outside the OI position.
  3. The two OBs rush through the gap between the OT and the OG on their side.
  4. The two DTs rush through the gap between the OG and CN on their side.
- Have the six players who are running the blitz charge hard up the field for 7 yards.

Special Teams Combination Drills

You may find that you have the time during the individual period to run special teams combination drills. But if your specialists in the kicking game are starting at other positions, you may need to conduct the following drills prior to the start of practice.

You may also find yourself in a situation where your practice field doesn't have a goal post for your placekicker (PK) to use. If you can establish some form of markers on the field to represent a straight line, then both kickers can use that as a reference point to determine if their kicks are traveling straight down the field.

The following drills use kicking across the field as a point of reference for you and your kickers. Kicking in this way allows the kickers to immediately see if the kicks are going to the right or left.

While these are combination drills, you can coach each position individually if you notice problems that need special work individually or with two players.

🏈 PUNTING

Number of players: Punter (P), long snapper (LN), and punt returners (PRs)
Equipment: Shorts or full pads, markers, ball
Time: 5 minutes/twice a week

1. The P, LN, and PRs line up in a straight line.
2. The coach establishes the distance from the ball to the P based on the LN's ability to make the long snap, keeping it in the LN's comfort range, especially in the beginning of the drill. Start at 10 yards and move back if he is able.
3. The coach establishes the PR's distance from the ball based on the distance of the P's kicks. Start close (20 yards) then move back (to 30 yards).
4. The LN concentrates on making an accurate snap.
5. The P focuses on catching the snap, taking the proper steps, kicking the ball straight, and not worrying about distance at the start of the drill.

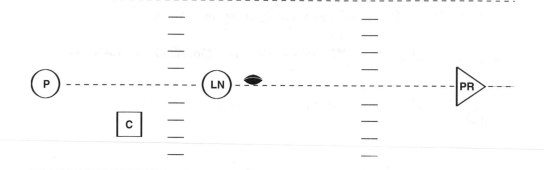

6. The PR focuses on moving under the punt and catching the ball in the air.

Coaching Points

- Check that the LN is in a correct stance:
    - His back is level and his head is up.
    - His feet are even and spread slightly wider than his shoulders. The ball is ahead of his shoulders.
    - His snapping hand grips the ball, with his fingers covering the laces of the ball in the same manner that a quarterback grips a ball to pass. His other hand rests lightly on the top of the ball.
- Next, check that the P is in a correct stance:
    - His feet are spread the width of his hips or slightly wider.
    - From this even-footed position, he takes a slight step forward with his punting foot, positioning the toe of his back foot even with the middle of his kicking foot. Check that his weight is on the balls of both feet.
    - He bends his knees slightly and brings his shoulders forward so they are a little in front of his hips.
    - His head is up with his eyes looking straight ahead.
- Finally check the stance of the PR:
    - He is standing upright, with his feet even and spread the width of his hips.
    - Both arms hang down in a relaxed manner.
    - His shoulders can be slightly in front of his hips.
    - He looks directly at the P so he can pick up the flight of the punt the moment it leaves the P's foot.
- Making the Snap:
    1. The LN has the ball turned so that the laces of the ball are on the side of his passing hand and near to the ground.
    2. Prior to the snap, he raises the front tip of the ball off the ground.
    3. He executes his snap with both hands back between his legs and extended toward the P.
    4. On release of the ball, the LN's hands rotate out to complete his snap.
- Kicking the Ball:
    1. The P establishes a target for the LN by extending his arms forward and positioning his hands so that his little fingers are together and his palms are up.
    2. Once he receives the ball, he holds it waist high, brings the laces to the top and begins his forward movement by taking a step with his kicking foot.
    3. On his second step, with his other foot, he lets the hand away from his kicking foot come off

Long snapper prepares to snap the ball to the punter

the ball and swing back to his side. The hand still on the ball is pushed forward and slightly outside his kicking foot, with the front point of the ball turned to the inside.

4. He has the ball level as he drops the ball to his foot.
5. His head and shoulders are in front of his hips as he brings his kicking leg up to meet the ball.

- Catching the Ball:
  1. The PR should have a clear view of the P. In a game, this will be more difficult because of the number of players on the line. The PR must understand that he should locate the ball as quickly as he can.
  2. While the ball is in the air, he moves so that he is directly in the path of the punt.
  3. As he comes under the ball, he has his little fingers together, palms up, and wrist cocked slightly down in position to receive the ball.
  4. He extends his arms so that he sees his hands and the ball at the moment of the catch.
  5. Once he makes the catch, the PR secures the ball and sprints up the field for 10 yards.
- Emphasize to the PR that he does not have to catch every punt. He can fair catch the punt and not advance it by waving one hand over his head prior to the catch, or he can allow the ball to roll dead. It will still be your team's possession.

🏈 PAT/FG

Number of players: Placekicker (PK), short snapper (SN), holder (H), and kick receiver (KR)
Equipment: Shorts or full pads, markers, ball, tee
Time: 5 minutes/twice a week

1. The PK, SN, H, and KR line up in a correct position.
2. The H gets into position 7 yards from the ball.

3. The coach establishes the KR's distance from the ball, based on the distance of the kicks. Start close (20 yards) then move back (to 30 yards).

4. During the drill, the SN concentrates on making the snap to the H. The H focuses on catching the snap and placing the ball on the tee. The PK concentrates on taking the proper steps, kicking the ball straight, and not worrying about distance at the start of the drill. The KR focuses on moving under the kick and catching the ball in the air.

Coaching Points

- The SN's stance:
  - His back is level and his head is up.
  - His feet are even and spread slightly wider than his shoulders. The ball is ahead of his shoulders.
  - His snapping hand grips the ball, with his fingers covering the laces of the ball in the same manner that a quarterback grips a ball to pass. His other hand rests lightly on the top of the ball.

Holder stance.

- The H's stance:
  - The H lines up on the opposite side of the tee from the PK.
  - He kneels down with his back knee on the ground, his other foot up and pointing straight ahead.
  - His shoulders are leaning forward.
- The PK's stance:
  - To find his proper alignment, the PK starts by facing the direction of the kick with his kicking foot immediately behind the tee and his plant foot even with and six inches away from his kicking foot.
  - He then backs away from the tee with three steps of normal length, then takes two steps sideways with his plant foot.
  - He faces the tee, starting in a correct stance with the heel of the plant foot just ahead of the toe of his kicking foot.
  - His feet are no wider than his hips, and his weight is distributed evenly on both feet.
  - Both knees are flexed, with his shoulders in front of his hips.
  - His arms are hanging down in a relaxed position.
  - He is looking at the tee, ready to move forward.

- The KR's stance:
  - The KR is standing upright with his feet even and spread the width of his hips.
  - Both arms hang down in a relaxed manner, and his shoulders are slightly in front of his hips.
  - He is looking directly at the PK so he can pick up the flight of the ball.
- Making the snap:
  1. The SN has the ball turned so that the laces of the ball are on the side of his passing hand and near to the ground.
  2. He looks back between his legs to be sure that the holder has his hands in position to catch the snap.
  3. He executes his snap with both hands back between his legs and extended toward the holder.
  4. On release of the ball, the SN's hands rotate out to complete his snap, and he sets up in position to block.

Holder and place kicker prepare for the snap.

- Placing the ball on the tee:
  1. The H places the hand nearest to the toe on the center of the tee and extends his other arm out at chest level toward the SN.
  2. He checks with the PK to see if he is in position to kick, then brings the hand from the tee up to the other hand. In this position, the H is telling the SN he is ready to receive the snap.
  3. The H's thumbs are together, and his wrists are cocked back.
  4. He catches the ball from the SN in his hands and brings it down to the tee.
  5. He then places the index finger of his hand nearest to the tee lightly on the top point of the ball, and using his other hand, he tries to spin the ball so the laces are pointing forward.
- Kicking the ball:
  1. As the ball is snapped, the PK takes a short step forward with his plant foot, followed by a normal step with his kicking foot and a final step with his plant foot so that it ends even with, and 6 inches outside of, the kicking tee.
  2. His hips and kicking leg rotate forward in a full arch, and his knee is ahead of his foot as he makes the kick.
  3. He points the toe of his kicking foot down and locks his ankle.
  4. The top inside center of his kicking foot makes contact 1 inch below the center of the ball.
  5. His body moves forward in a straight line following his kick.
- Catching the ball:
  1. Prior to the snap, the KR focuses on the tee and tries to pick up the flight of the ball the instant it leaves the PK's foot.
  2. With the ball in the air, the KR moves in front of the path of the ball and adjusts his position so that he is actually moving forward as he makes the catch.

ST PAT/FG

Short snapper, holder, and place-kicker in their stances.

3. The ball should be coming end-over-end, so the KR must have his little fingers together, palms up, and elbows close to his sIdes.
4. As he approaches the ball, he reaches out with both hands and is in position to see both his hands and the ball at the moment of the catch.
5. He immediately secures the ball to his side, runs hard up the field for 10 yards, then jogs the ball back to the SN.

KICKOFF

Number of players: Kicker (K) and kick receiver (KR)
Equipment: Shorts or full pads, ball, tee
Time: 5 minutes/twice a week

1. The K and KR line up in their correct positions.
2. The kicker places the ball correctly on the tee before moving into position.
3. The coach establishes the distance of the KR from the ball based on the distance of the kicks. Start close (20 to 25 yards) then move back (35 or 40 yards).
4. Once everyone is set, the coach yells "Go," and the K approaches and kicks the ball, with the KR catching the ball and running it back to the K.
5. The drill is repeated.

Coaching Points

- The K's stance:
  - The K gets into the correct stance by starting with his kicking foot directly behind the ball and tee and his other foot at the side of the tee.
  - He then steps away from the tee with his kicking foot, turns his back to the tee, and takes eight normal steps away from the ball.
  - Next he turns to face the tee again and takes five steps to the side of his plant foot, turning back to face the tee and the ball at a 45-degree angle.
- The KR's stance:
  - The KR is standing upright, with his feet even and spread the width of his hips.
  - Both arms hang down in a relaxed manner, and his shoulders are slightly in front of his hips.
  - He is looking directly at the K and the tee so that he can pick up the flight of the ball the instant it leaves the tee.
- Kicking the ball:
  1. The K has his plant foot a half step ahead of his kicking foot, with his shoulders in front of his hips, knees bent slightly, and arms hanging down in a relaxed manner.
  2. On the command of "Go," the K takes a short half step forward with his plant foot, then controlled steps to the ball for the first 5 yards.
  3. He quickens his pace for the final approach to the tee and prepares to attack the ball.
  4. His plant foot hits the ground 6 inches outside the ball and 3 inches behind the tee. He has his head down looking at the ball and the tee as he brings his kicking leg through to the ball.
  5. His hips and kicking leg rotate forward in a full arch, and his knee is ahead of his foot as he makes the kick.
  6. He points the toe of his kicking foot down and locks his ankle.
  7. The top inside center of his kicking foot makes contact 1 inch below the center of the ball.
  8. The motion of the kick allows his body to move forward in a straight line following his kick.
- Catching the ball:
  1. Prior to the kick, the KR focuses on the tee and tries to pick up the flight of the ball the instant it leaves the K's foot.
  2. With the ball in the air, the KR moves in front of the path of the ball and tries to adjust his position so that he is actually moving forward as he makes the catch.
  3. The ball should be coming end-over-end, so the KR must have his little fingers together, palms up, and elbows close to his sides.
  4. As he approaches the ball, he reaches out with both hands and is in position to see both his hands and the ball at the moment of the catch.
  5. He immediately secures the ball to his side, runs hard up the field for 10 yards, and jogs the ball back to the K.
- Emphasize to the KR that a kickoff is different from a punt in that a kickoff is a *free ball* and must be caught or fallen on, or the other team can recover the kick and gain possession of the ball.

Kicker stance.

PERIOD 3
Group Practice

Passing Drills

It is really important to understand that competition can and will surface when you plan and implement the following types of drills. This competition can be used as a fun way to motivate your players as well as provide you with a record of your individual players' performances if you decide to keep a written record each practice.

WIDE RECEIVER, TIGHT END, QUARTERBACKS AND DEFENSIVE BACKS PASSING

Number of players: QBs, WRs, TEs, and DBs
Equipment: Full pads, marker, ball
Time: 10 minutes/once a week

1. Four offensive receivers, the QB, and four defensive players line up on the field. The other three defensive backs move up to the line until it is their turn to cover.
2. The coach designates which WR and TE is to run the route and which defensive back is to have the coverage.
3. The QB tells the WR and TE the route to run.
4. The coach tells the defender the coverage to use.
5. On the snap count of "Hut," the QB takes his correct drop, the WR and TE run their routes, and the defensive backs maks the coverage.
6. After the play, the WR and TE return the ball to the QB.
7. The drill is repeated using a new WR, TE, and defensive backs.

Coaching Points
- Have players change position once all four players have had a turn.

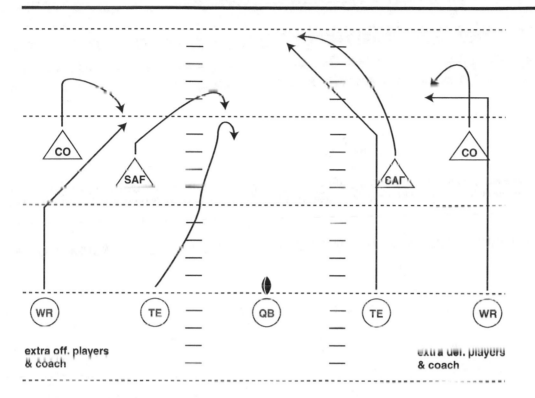

extra off. players
& coach

extra def. players
& coach

- Check that the participating players start correctly on the snap.
- Make certain that the QB takes the proper steps in his drop, uses a correct throwing motion, and delivers the ball on time.
- Check that the receiver runs the route at the proper depth and has his hands in the correct position to make the catch.
- Check to see that the defensive man is in a good backpedal, is focused on the receiver, correctly leaves his backpedal, and takes the proper path to cause an incompletion or make an interception.
- Make your corrections when the players are not involved in the drill.

This same type of drill can be set up to aid the running backs in learning their pass routes and to teach the linebackers the techniques needed to play man-to-man pass defense.

RUNNING BACKS AND QUARTERBACKS, AND LINEBACKER PASSING

Number of players: QBs, RBs, and LBs
Equipment: Full pads, marker, ball
Time: 10 minutes/once a week

1. Two RBs, the QB, and three linebackers line up on the field.

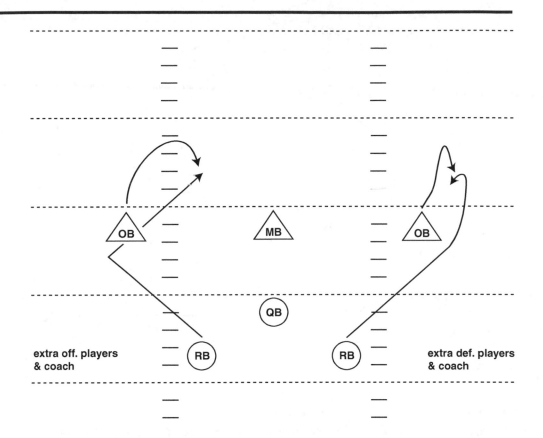

2. The coach designates which RB is to run the route and which linebacker is to have coverage. The linebackers not in the drill move up to the line and take a knee.
3. The QB tells the RB the route to run.
4. The coach tells the linebacker the coverage to use.
5. On the snap count of "Hut," the QB takes his correct drop, the RB runs his route, and the linebacker makes the coverage.
6. After the play, the RB returns the ball to the QB.
7. The drill is repeated using a new RB and linebacker.

Coaching Points

- Players change position once all the players have had a turn.
- Check that the players start correctly on the snap.
- Make certain that the QB takes the proper steps in his drop, uses a correct throwing motion, and delivers the ball on time.
- Check that the RB runs the route at the proper depth and that his hands are in the correct position to make the catch.
- Check to see that the linebacker is in a good backpedal, is focused on the RB, leaves his backpedal correctly, and takes the proper path to cause an incompletion or make an interception.

- Make your corrections when the players are not involved in the drill.

The next group of passing drills involves an entire set of eligible receivers and the quarterback versus a set of linebackers and defensive backs. Often this drill is referred to as a *skeleton passing drill* in that only the offensive and defensive linemen are absent from the drill. This drill is different from the previous two. Now all the receivers are running routes at the same time, and the entire defensive group is involved in coverage.

Try to have your offensive and defensive calls scripted so the drill can proceed as quickly as possible. Make any corrections to players when they are not involved in the drill.

WIDE RECEIVERS, TIGHT ENDS, RUNNING BACKS, QUARTERBACKS, LINEBACKERS, AND DEFENSIVE BACKS PASSING

Number of players: QBs, WRs, TEs, RBs, LBs, and DBs
Equipment: Full pads, marker, ball
Time: 10 minutes/once a week

1. Six offensive and seven defensive players line up on the field.
2. The QB huddles the offensive personnel and gives them the pass play and the snap count. Remind the QB which player is the primary receiver and which is the secondary for the pass play called.
3. The defensive team huddles up and the middle linebacker (MB) gives them the coverage to use.
4. The players then line up.
5. On the snap count of "Hut," the QB takes his drop, the offensive players run their pass routes, and the defensive players drop into the designated coverage.
6. After the play, the receiver making the catch returns the ball to the QB.
7. The drill is repeated using a new group of offensive and defensive players.

Coaching Points

- Have each group run three plays.
- Offensive players change their formations and pass routes based on the play called by the coach.
- Check that all the participating players start correctly on the snap.
- Make certain that the QB takes the proper steps in his drop, uses a correct throwing motion, and delivers the ball on time.
- Check that each receiver runs the correct route at the proper depth, has his hands in the correct

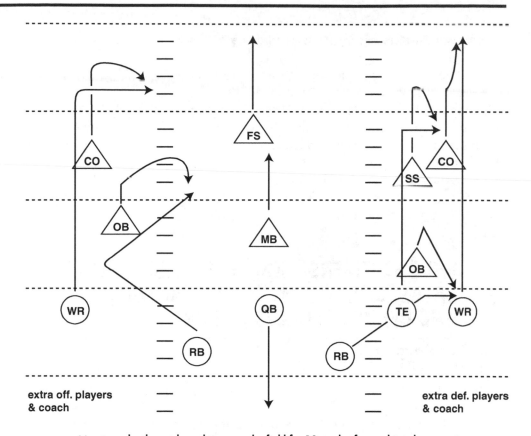

extra off. players
& coach

extra def. players
& coach

position to make the catch, and turns up the field for 10 yards after making the reception.
- Check that all the defensive players play the coverage called, using correct technique for that coverage, and rally to the ball once the pass is thrown.
- Make your corrections when the players are not involved in the drill.

During this drill, try to have the offense run pass routes at all depths and force the quarterback to use his proper drop. You can tell the quarterback prior to the beginning of each pass play who his primary and secondary receivers are and coach him to think of throwing the ball to the receiver that is the most open.

In a same manner, you can vary the defensive coverage on each play so that your defensive team gets the experience of running each coverage. This approach presents a different look for the offensive players.

Pass Protection
and Rush Drills

You can bring your offensive and defensive linemen together while the other players are working on offensive and defensive pass plays. This will provide you with an opportunity to focus on the techniques needed to pass protect and to rush the passer.

 ## OFFENSIVE AND DEFENSIVE LINE PASS PROTECTION AND RUSH

Number of players: All OLs and DLs
Equipment: Full pads, marker
Time: 10 minutes/once a week

1. Five offensive linemen and five defensive linemen line up on the field.
2. The coach places a marker to designate where the QB will set up.
3. The coach designates which two players will be involved in the drill at one time, matching up players of equal size and ability as much as possible.
4. For the defensive linemen, the coach establishes where their rush lane is, either inside or outside the offensive blocker.
5. On the command of "Hut," the CN simulates a snap with the ball.
6. With the snap the offensive lineman sets back to pass protect and the defensive lineman moves forward to rush the passer.
7. After three or four seconds, the coach blows a whistle or calls "Stop" to end the drill.
8. The next two players line up and repeat the drill.
9. After all the offensive and defensive linemen have drilled twice, substitutes can be made and the drill can go again.

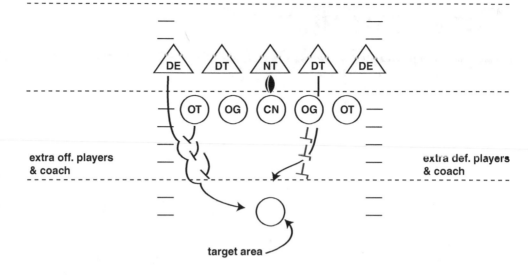

target area

Coaching Points

- If the CN is involved in the drill, it is good to have another offensive lineman line up as the QB and take the snap so that the ball is not on the ground.
- Prior to the snap, make certain that each offensive lineman knows where the coach will be setting up the QB target area for the drill.
- Also prior to the snap, check with each defensive lineman on what technique he plans to use to reach the target area.
- Check that the defensive lineman is looking in at the ball for his signal to start his rush.
- Make certain that each offensive player is using the correct pass protection technique, and each defensive player is using the proper pass rush technique during the drill.
- Make your corrections when the players are not involved in the drill.

This is also a time when you have the opportunity to focus on your linebackers blitzing and your running backs working on their pass protection blocking. Keep a written record of which players successfully complete their assignments.

🏈 RUNNING BACKS AND LINEBACKERS PASS PROTECTION AND RUSH

Number of players: RBs and LBs
Equipment: Full pads, marker
Time: 10 minutes/once a week

1. Two RBs and four linebackers (2 OBs and 2 IBs) line up on the field.
2. The coach places a marker to designate where the QB will set up—the target area.

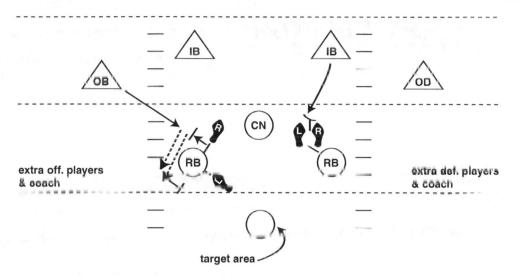

extra off. players
& coach

extra def. players
& coach

target area

3. The coach designates which two players will be involved in the drill at one time, matching up players of equal size and ability.
4. The coach establishes the rush lane for the linebackers (i.e., either inside or outside the offensive blocker).
5. On the command of "Hut," the CN (can be an extra running back) simulates a snap with the ball.
6. With the snap the RB sets up to pass protect and the linebacker moves forward to rush the passer.
7. After three or four seconds, the coach blows a whistle or calls "Stop" to end the drill.
8. The next two players line up and repeat the drill.
9. After both RBs have blocked both an inside and outside pass rusher, and all four LBs have had two opportunities to rush, substitutes can be made and the drill can go again.

Coaching Points

- Prior to the snap, make certain that each RB knows where the QB will be setting up for the drill.
- Prior to the snap, check with each linebacker to determine which technique he plans to use to reach the target area.
- Check that the linebacker is looking in at the ball for his signal to start the rush.
- Make certain that each RB is using the correct pass protection technique, and each linebacker is using the proper pass rush technique during the drill.
- Make your corrections when the players are not involved in the drill.

Weak-Side Drill

This is an excellent type of drill when you have limited players, do not want to have a full team practice, or want to focus all of your attention on the offensive and defensive players on one side of the formation. You can predetermine the running and passing plays that you will feature to this side of your formation and the defenses that your team will use.

🏈 WEAK SIDE

Number of players: QBs, WRs, OLs, RBs, DLs, LBs, and DBs
Equipment: Full pads, ball
Time: 10 minutes/once a week

1. The seven offensive and six defensive players line up in their positions on the field.
2. The QB huddles the offensive personnel and gives them the formation, play, and snap count. The QB then breaks the huddle and brings the offensive players to the line.
3. The defensive team huddles up and the middle linebacker (MB) gives them the defense they will run.
4. The players line up appropriately.
5. On the snap count, the offensive players try to run the play called, and the defensive players try to stop the play by executing the defense called.
6. Each group of offensive players has four plays before the coach substitutes new groups for the drill.
7. The coach changes the formation (the alignment of the backs) based on the play called in the huddle.
8. In this type of drill, offensive plays might include:
   - Slant play (as diagrammed): The tailback (TB) runs outside the OT with the fullback (FB) blocking out on the OB.

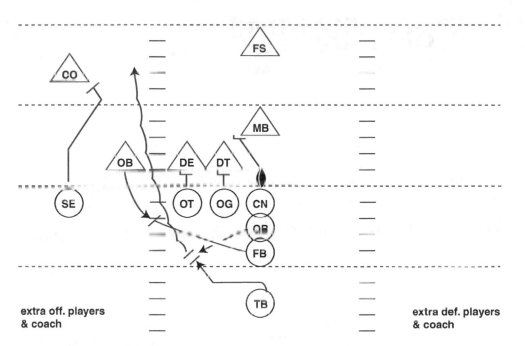

extra off. players
& coach

extra def. players
& coach

- Pitch play: The ball is pitched back to the TB, with the SE blocking in on the OB and the FB leading wide up the field to the outside to block the CO or safety.
- Option play: The QB comes down the line, faking to the FB inside the OT, then either pitches the ball to the TB if the LB attacks him or keeps the ball if he widens out and turns up inside the OB.
- Drop-back pass play: The QB throws to either the halfback (HB) or the split end (SE) based on the pass pattern called in the huddle.
- All the running plays could be run with straight-ahead blocking by the three offensive linemen.

9. The defensive calls might include a base defense with:
- A man-to-man coverage
- A 2-deep zone coverage
- A 3-deep zone coverage
- A blitz coverage with either the MB or OB blitzing on the snap

Coaching Points
- Make sure all the players are lined up in their positions and no one is offsides on the play.
- Check that every player in the drill is executing his assignment using the proper technique.
- Make certain that the QB carries out his fake after handing or pitching the ball to the TB.
- Allow the play to continue until the ball carrier is tackled or runs out of bounds, or the pass is incomplete. To get the players conditioned to stop in a game, blow a whistle to end the play.
- Make your corrections when the players are not involved in the drill.
- Let all the players have a chance to run a left offensive side drill, then substitute players and run the drill to the right side.

Strong-Side Drill

When setting up your strong-side drill, it is very important to take into consideration the base offense that you will be teaching to your players. If you feature a two–wide receiver offense you will need to involve the flanker in this drill. For those teams that feature a wing-T attack and formation (and I realize that many coaches use this attack), you will have to incorporate a wingback in the drill. The defense should be prepared to line up and adjust to the formation the offense uses.

STRONG SIDE

Number of players: QBs, WRs, OLs, RBs, DLs, LBs, and DBs
Equipment: Full pads, ball
Time: 10 minutes/once a week

1. The eight offensive and six defensive players line up in their positions on the field.
2. The QB huddles the offensive personnel and gives them the formation, play, and snap count. The QB breaks the huddle and brings the offensive players to the line.
3. The defensive team huddles up and the middle linebacker (MB) gives them the defense they will run.
4. All players line up according to their plays.
5. On the snap count, the offensive players run the play called, and the defensive players execute the defense called to stop the play.
6. The coach gives each group of offensive players four plays before substituting new groups for the drill.
7. The coach changes the formation (the alignment of the backs) based on the play called in the huddle.

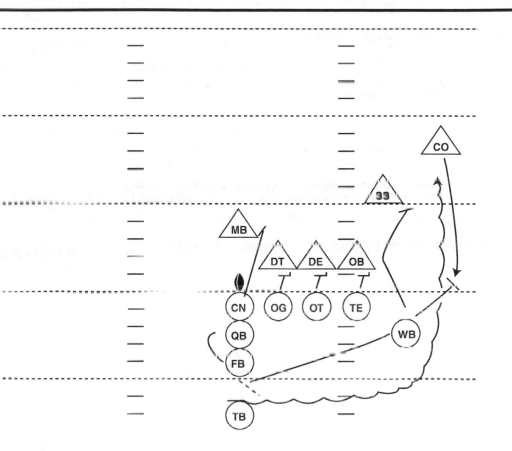

8. In this type of drill, offensive plays might include:
   - Power off-tackle play: The TB runs outside the OT. The TE and OT double team the defensive end, with the FB blocking out on the OB and the WB stepping at the OB, then driving up the field to block the SS.
   - Pitch play (as diagrammed above): The ball is pitched back to the TB. The WB blocks on the SS, the FB leads up the field on the CO, and all other players block the men in front of them.
   - Option play: The QB comes down the line, fakes to the FB inside the OT, then either pitches the ball to the TB if the LB attacks him, or keeps the ball if he widens out and turns up inside the OB. The TE releases inside the OB and helps the CN block the MB. The WB fakes to the inside on the OB, then releases outside of him to block the SS.
   - Drop-back pass: The QB throws to either the TE, wingback/flanker back, or RB, based on the pass pattern called in the huddle.
   - The running plays could be run with straight ahead blocking by the three OLs except in the case of the double team block.
9. The defensive calls might include a base defense with:
   - A man-to-man coverage
   - A 2-deep zone coverage

- A 3-deep zone coverage
- A blitz coverage with either the MB or OB blitzing on the snap

Coaching Points

- Make certain that all the players are lined up correctly, and no one is offsides on the play.
- Make certain that the QB carries out his fake after handing or pitching the ball to the TB.
- Allow the play to continue until the ball carrier is tackled or runs out of bounds, or until the pass is incomplete. To get the players conditioned to stop in a game, blow a whistle to end the play.
- Make your corrections when the players are not involved in the drill.
- Let all the players run a right side drill, then substitute players and run the drill going to the left side.

PERIOD 4
Special Teams

Punt Coverage and Punt Return

When working with any section of the kicking game, it is important to start simple, then introduce any variations that can become a part of your special teams.

In dealing with your punt team, there are four fundamentals that need to be practiced:

1. Your center snap is accurate.
2. The punter makes the catch and gets the punt off properly.
3. The blockers focus on protecting the punter until the ball leaves his foot.
4. Your players cover the kick and do not allow a long return.

PUNT COVERAGE

Number of players: Punt team
Equipment: Shorts or full pads, markers, ball
Time: 5 minutes/once a week

1. The entire punt return team and the punt team line up in their assigned positions.
2. The blockers get in their 2-point stance.
3. The CN looks back between his legs and sees that the P is ready.
4. Once the ball is snapped, the blockers hold their position until the ball is kicked.
5. The two outside players look in at the ball and sprint off the line when the ball is snapped.
6. Each player sprints down the field and maintains proper position on the return man.

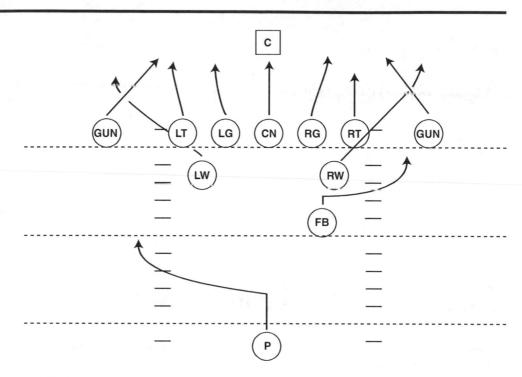

7. After the team covers the kick, they move to the sideline and another group of players take their place.

Coaching Points

- Check that the CN has a proper grip on the ball with both hands.
- Make certain the P is at the correct depth and signals the CN that he is ready by extending both hands with his palms up and little fingers together.
  - The linemen and wingbacks get in a 2-point stance with their back foot back and their weight on their front foot. On the snap, they push back, take a position to block for at least two counts, and sprint down the field on the kick.
  - The two outside players (the gunners) sprint directly at the return man and begin to shorten and widen their stride. They get into a position to tackle when they are within 5 yards of the PR.
  - Make certain the players on both sides of the ball widen out as they release and keep the ball on their inside shoulder as they run down the field.
  - The CN tries to go directly at the return man.
  - The FB moves to the right side of the field and acts as a safety.
  - After executing the punt, the P moves to the left side of the field and acts as the safety on that side.
  - Instruct the players who are not on the punt team that a punt is not a free ball. It can only be downed. It cannot be recovered unless it first hits a member of the punt return team.
  - Once you feel that your punt coverage team is working well together, you might want to add:

Center prepares to snap the ball to the punter.

ST Punt Coverage

- A *pass* to the FB in the right flat if your P can pass the ball.
- A *run* to the left by the FB, with both wingbacks leading around the LT. The CN needs to snap the ball directly to the FB.
- You might consider either of the above plays if you are punting from your opponent's side of the 50-yard line.

PUNT PROTECTION

Number of players: 8 punt blockers and 7 punt rushers
Equipment: Shorts or full pads, markers, ball
Time: 2 minutes/once a week

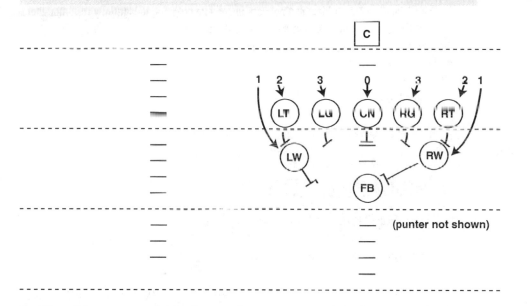

(punter not shown)

1. The eight punt team blockers and seven punt rushers line up in their correct positions.
2. The blockers get in their correct stances, and the rush men get in a 3-point stance looking in at the ball.
3. The player lined up in the P's position signals the CN he is ready for the snap, and the CN then snaps the ball.
4. On the snap the blockers should set back off the line and block the rushers as they come across.
5. Each group blocks twice as a team, then another group of players goes through the drill.

Coaching Points

- In the beginning of the year, you may want to only rush one player at a time until all the blockers master the correct technique.

- Because we are only concerned with the punt blocking, it is not necessary to punt the ball or for the blockers to cover down the field.
- Punt Protection:
  1. On the snap, the blocker sets back off the line.
  2. The blocker has his knees bent and his hands up in front of his chest. He keeps shuffling his feet as he sets off the line.
  3. The blocker strikes the rush man in the chest with the palms of both hands to stop his progress to the P.
  4. If the man he is blocking tries to go to the inside, the blocker must drop his inside foot back, hit the rush man in the chest, and drive him to the inside across the formation.
  5. Each blocker stays with his man for two counts, then releases down the field for three or four steps.
  6. The FB should set in position, and not back up, and be prepared to block any rush man that is free. He also needs to look from the center to the outside.
- Blocking assignments (as shown on diagram):
  #1 LW and RW
  #2 LT and RT
  #3 LG and RG
  #0 CN
  —FB (free; can block anyone)

🏈 RIGHT PUNT RETURN

Number of players: Punt and punt return players
Equipment: Shorts or full pads, markers, ball
Time: 5 minutes/once a week

1. The entire punt return team and the punt team line up in their positions.
2. The blockers get in their correct stance, and the down rush men get in a 3-point stance looking in at the ball.
3. The player lined up in the P's position signals the CN he is ready for the snap. The CN then snaps the ball.
4. On the snap the blockers should set back off the line and block the rushers as they come across.
5. The rushers should move into the blockers and keep them on the line of scrimmage.

Coaching Points

- In this drill, we are concerned with holding the coverage men on the line, then once the ball is kicked, setting up our blocking for a return up the right side of the field.
- Have each group rush and set up twice as a team before substituting another group of players into the drill.
- Instruct the P to try to punt the ball down the center of the field.

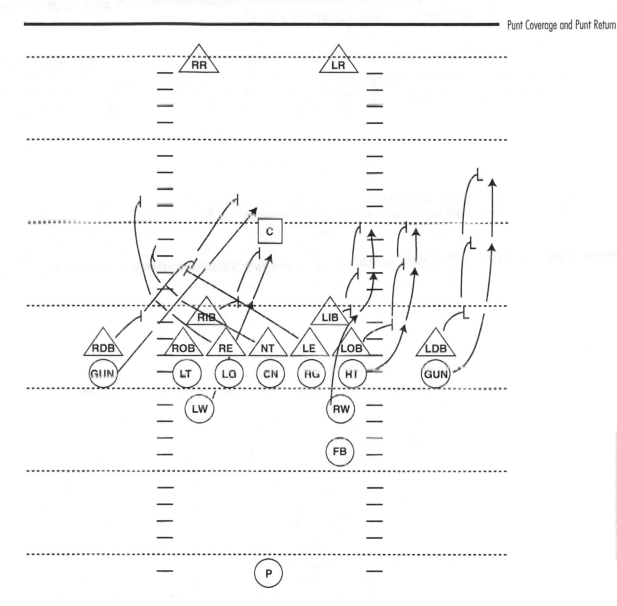

- Both the right defensive back and left defensive back need to step into the gunner on their side, try to keep him on the line, then run with him down the field. The RDB forces his gunner to the center of the field, while the LDB forces his gunner to the sideline.
- Both OBs step into the tackle on their side and push the blocker as far back into the backfield as they can. Then they run with the player down the field. The ROB forces his tackle into the center of the field, while the LOB forces his tackle to the sideline.
- Both ends step into the guard on their side, push them as far back into the backfield as they can, then force the blocker to release on their left side. The RE then sprints downfield 15 yards to the right and should be the first man on the wall on the hash mark, ready to block any opponent that shows. The LE sprints downfield 5 yards and should be the third man on the wall on the hash mark, ready to block any opponent that shows.
- If allowed by the rules in your league, the NT tries to get both hands on the CN, thus keeping him

on the line and forcing him to release to his left side. Then the NT sprints downfield 10 yards and should be the second man on the wall on the hash mark, ready to block any opponent that shows.

- Both IBs focus on the wingman on their side and are prepared to step in front of him, regardless of how he tries to release, and to stay with him during the entire play. The RIB should try to force the wing on his side into the center of the field, and the LIB should try to force his wing to the sideline.
- Make certain that all the players near the line of scrimmage keep working toward the P until they are certain that the ball is kicked.
- Both the right and left return men should quickly call out who is going to catch the punt. The catcher calls out "I've got it," and his partner answers "Yours, yours."
- The return man not making the catch moves slightly in front of his partner, calls out if he needs to make a fair catch on short or high kicks, looks back to make certain the ball is caught, then leads up the field to the right, aiming for a position outside the wall. He should be prepared to block the first opponent who shows, and if none appears, he continues running up the field.
- The return man with the ball listens for a fair catch call, focuses on the flight of the ball, gets in position to correctly make the catch, drives straight up the field for 5 yards, breaks to the right, and follows his partner up the field.
- Remember to tell the punt return team that once the ball is kicked it's going to be your ball even if no one catches the punt.
- Instruct all blockers that they must block in the front or on the side—not in the back—and they cannot hold on the return.
- For a left return, teach your players to hold up the same men but reverse the side that they want to force them to release to once the kick is made.
- For a punt rush, where you want to try to block the punt, you can have the down players on the line rush through the inside gap of the man in front of them using a crossover step with their outside foot and ripping up with their outside arm.
- When rushing the P to block a punt, make certain that all rush men aim for a spot 3 yards in front of the P's original position, and that they cross their arms in front of their face when they go to block the punt. Be sure they keep their eyes on the ball as they approach the P, and they are ready to leave their feet if necessary.
- Usually you will only want to rush the three players on the side of the ball away from the return. This is so the players do not run into one another, yet you still have a good chance for a return.
- Emphasize to every rush player that he must avoid touching the punter, and if the punt is blocked and does not cross the line of scrimmage, he can pick the ball up and run it in for a touchdown.

Kickoff and Kickoff Return Drills

KICKOFF

Number of players: Kickoff and kickoff return players
Equipment: Shorts or full pads, ball
Time: 5 minutes/once a week

1. The ten coverage players and the K get in their proper positions on the field.
2. The coach sets up a group of nine players in return positions and two kick returners to catch the ball and bring it up the field.
3. The coach tells the players on the return team who they are to block and where the ball will be returned.
4. On the whistle, the K kicks the ball, and the coverage players move down the field to make their coverage.
5. Every coverage person should try to touch the ball carrier. It is not necessary to have the coverage players tackle the ball carrier as long as they are in position to make the tackle.
6. The coverage team exits on the sideline so the next group of players on the coverage team can line up for the next kick.

Coaching Points

- Make certain that all coverage players are moving with the K and are in a full run at the moment of the kick.
- Check that each player stays in his assigned coverage lane and is sprinting down the field.
- Coach the players to avoid blockers and quickly get back into their coverage lane.
- Emphasize that the players need to shorten their stride, come under control, and prepare to make the tackle on the return man.
- Check that the K and the safeties are in position to stop any long return.

ST Kickoff

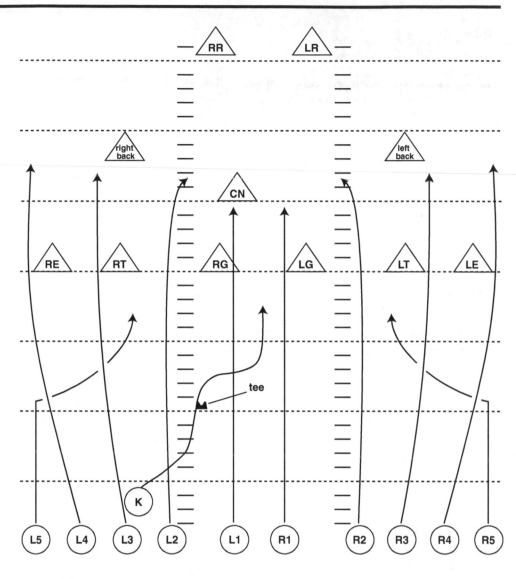

🏈 MIDDLE KICKOFF

Number of players: All kickoff and kickoff return players
Equipment: Shorts or full pads, ball
Time: 5 minutes/once a week

1. The coach sets up a group of nine players in return positions and two kick returners to catch the kicked ball and bring it up the field.
2. The ten coverage players and the K get in their positions on the field.
3. The coach tells the players on the return team who they are to block and shows them where the ball will be returned on the middle return.
4. On the whistle, the K kicks the ball, and the coverage players move down the field to make their coverage.

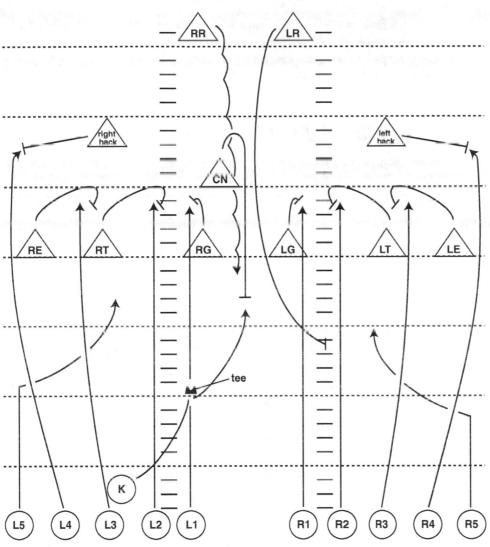

Middle Kickoff

5. Each blocker drops back and locates the cover player he is to block.

6. Each blocker tries to stay with his man until the play ends.

7. The coverage team should allow the blockers to make their block and the return man to run up the field.

8. After the return, a new group of players quickly line up to run the next return.

Coaching Points

- Make certain that the front line of blockers holds their position until they are certain the ball has been kicked down the field.
- Check that each blocker drops back at the correct angle and moves into the proper position to make his block.
- Emphasize that the players need to shorten their stride, come under control, lower their hips,

bring their hands up in front of their chest with palms forward, and be prepared to make the block on the coverage man.

- Check that the returner moves in front of the ball, catches it in stride, then following the other returner, runs straight up the field.

ONSIDE KICKOFF

Number of players: KO and KR players
Equipment: Shorts or full pads, markers, ball
Time: 5 minutes/once a week

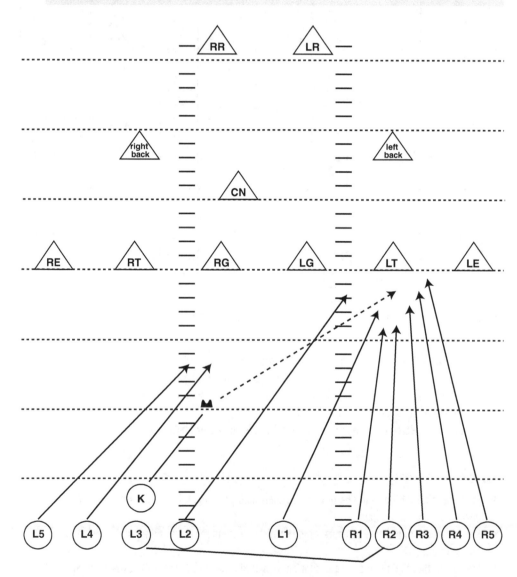

1. The ten coverage players and the K get in their proper positions on the field.
2. The coach sets up a group of nine players in return positions and two kick returners to catch the kicked ball and bring it up the field.
3. The coach instructs the players on the return team to drop back as the K approaches the ball.
4. The coach alerts the kicking team as to where the onside kick will be directed.
5. On the whistle, the K kicks the ball, and the coverage players move forward, prepared to recover the ball.
6. Every coverage player should try to recover the ball if possible.
7. Players who cannot recover the ball should block players on the return team.
8. The coverage team exits on the sideline so the next group of players on the coverage team can line up for the next onside kick.

Coaching Points

- Make certain that all the coverage players are moving with the K and are in a full run at the moment of the kick.
- Check that each coverage player is looking at the ball as he sprints to recover the kick after the ball has gone 10 yards or has been touched by an opposing player.
- Coach the players to block if they cannot get to the ball.
- Emphasize that the K needs to hit the top half of the ball on the kick so that the ball stays on the ground and has a chance to bounce.
- If the RB and LB are dropping into the center of the field prior to the kick, you may consider a short high kick, or *pooch kick*, to the sideline behind the front line of the return team. The K should hit the ball low and lift it high into the air.

"HANDS" KICKOFF RETURN

Number of players: KO and KR players
Equipment: Shorts or full pads, markers, ball
Time: 5 minutes/once a week

1. To defend against an onside kick, the coach sets up a group of nine players in return positions and two kick returners.
2. The coach instructs the players on the return team to hold their positions and be prepared to fall on the ball if it is kicked in their direction.
3. The coach informs the kicking team where the onside kick will be directed.
4. On the whistle, the K kicks the ball, and the coverage players move forward to recover the ball.
5. Players on the return team who cannot recover the ball should

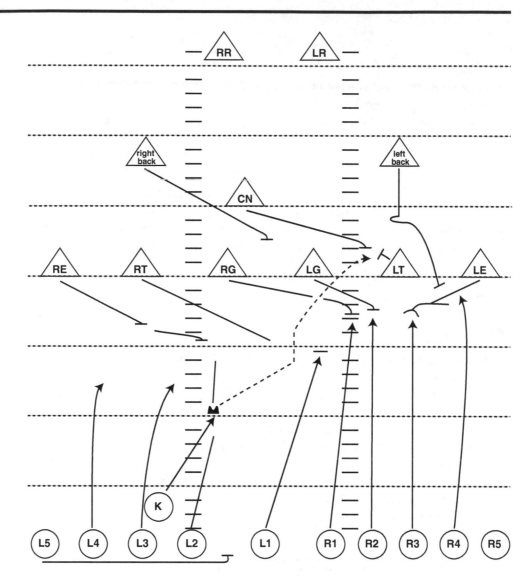

immediately block any player on the coverage team who is near the ball.

6. The return team exits on the sideline so that the next group of players on the return team can line up for the next onside kick attempt.

Coaching Points

- Make certain that all the return players hold their positions and focus on the flight of the ball.
- Check that the RB and LB have moved up into a position to catch a pooch kick or a high bouncing kick. Inform them that they can signal for a fair catch if it is a high kick in the air.
- Coach the return players to move forward to block if they cannot get to the ball.
- Emphasize that a kickoff is a free ball, and, as such, it can be recovered by players from either team.
- If the ball is kicked deep to the return men, the blockers should automatically run a middle return.

PAT/FG and Field Goal Block

There are four factors to consider when deciding whether or not to kick following a touchdown or trying for a field goal:

1. Can your center make a snap that is accurate?
2. Do you have a holder who can catch the snap and place the ball down correctly in the proper position?
3. Is there a player on your team who has the ability to successfully make the kick?
4. Can your blockers successfully keep the rush players from blocking the kick?

PAT/FG KICK

Number of players: PAT/FG and PAT/FG block teams
Equipment: Shorts or full pads, ball
Time: 5 minutes/once a week

1. Both the kicking and blocking teams line up in their assigned positions.
2. The H asks the PK if he is ready.
3. The H signals the CN that he is ready for the snap by reaching out with both hands to give the CN the target.
4. The CN looks back between his legs, sees the target, knows the H and PK are ready, and makes the snap.
5. On the snap, all the blockers set to block.
6. The PK must concentrate on the tee, the ball, and making the kick.
7. If trying to kick a field goal, the blockers must fan out after the kick because the opposing team can run the ball back if the kick is short.
8. One team attempts three kicks, then a new group comes in and repeats the drill.

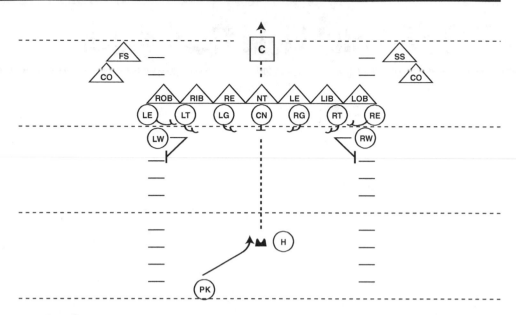

Coaching Points

- When first working on the kick, have the rush people come in hard for only two steps and allow the kick to be made.
- Check that the CN has a good stance, grips the ball properly, follows through with both hands on the snap, and comes up to help block.
- Make certain the H is in good position and is ready to catch the snap regardless of where it is. Also as he places the ball on the tee, be sure he spins the ball so that the laces are facing forward.
- The PK should be positioned correctly, take the appropriate steps, and use a good kicking motion as he makes his kick. Check that he is coming forward and not falling back as he kicks the ball.

PAT/FG lineup.

- Make certain that the ends, tackles, and guards all step back and to the inside with their inside foot, bring both hands up to the center of their chest, extend their elbows to the outside, and block the inside gap first
- Both wingmen need to bring their hands up to their chests, bend their knees, keep their heads up and be ready to block the first rush man that shows up outside of the end on their side.
- Instruct every member on the kicking team that if the kick is blocked, they must tackle any opposing player who picks it up.
- When the snap is bad, the H must be prepared to get up and run with the ball, with the PK serving as his blocker.
- If the H can throw, you might want to have some form of rollout pass where the H will secure the ball and move toward the sideline either to his right or left to either pass or run the ball, with the two eligible receivers on the side of the rollout running pass routes. The wing runs to the corner, and the end blocks, then runs into the flat. The PK swings down the other side to get a throw-back pass.

At first you may find it challenging to put together the specialists needed for a successful PAT/FG team. However, if the rules under which your team plays give a point increase for a kicked PAT, it will be advantageous if you can make it work.

When working on the block, it is often better to begin by having the players rush individually first, then in small groups. You can usually divide your rush team into three-man groups, starting with the two defensive ends and the nose tackle in the middle for an inside rush and the corner and two backers on either side for your outside rush. It is better to bring an outside rush from only one side at a time, because there is always the possibility that the rushing players may collide.

PAT/FG BLOCK MIDDLE

Number of players: PAT/FG and PAT/FG block teams
Equipment: Shorts or full pads, ball
Time: 5 minutes/once a week

1. Both the kicking and the blocking teams line up in their proper positions.
2. The seven front line players on the block team line up in a 3-point stance looking in at the ball.
3. On the snap, the two ends and the NT rush up the center with the IBs rushing between the end and tackle, while the two OBs rush outside the wings and make sure the ball is kicked.
4. One team attempts to block three kicks, then a new group comes in and repeats the drill.

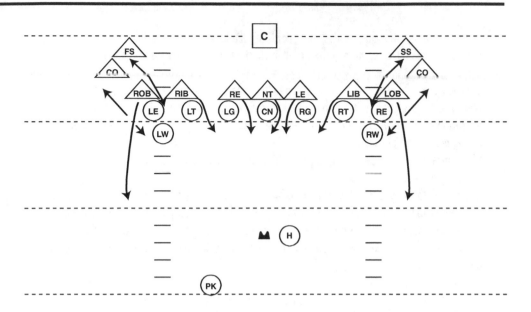

Coaching Points

- Check that all seven frontline players move on the snap of the ball.
- Make certain that the two ends direct their charge through the inside shoulder of each offensive guard, and that the NT directs his charge through the shoulder of the CN on the wide side of the field.
- These three players need to drive hard for three steps, then extend their arms up and try to jump in the air to deflect the ball.
- Check that the IBs are charging through the gap between the guard and tackle on their respective sides, and trying to penetrate to a spot 2 yards in front of the tee to make the block.
- Both OBs rush outside the wing on their side, come up the field 5 yards, and prepare to tackle the ball carrier if the ball is not kicked, or recover the ball when it is blocked.
- Check that each CO focuses on and covers the wingback on his side until the ball is kicked.
- Make certain that both safeties focus on and take coverage on the end on their side until the ball is kicked.
- Alert the members of the block team that if the ball is blocked and does not cross the line of scrimmage, they can pick it up and run for a touchdown.
- Emphasize to all the players on the block team that if the field goal is short, they do not have to recover the ball. They can allow it to roll dead, and it will still be their ball.
- Remind all players that they must avoid touching the PK as they make their rush.

PAT/FG BLOCK RIGHT

Number of players: PAT/FG and PAT/FG block teams
Equipment: Shorts or full pads, ball
Time: 5 minutes/once a week

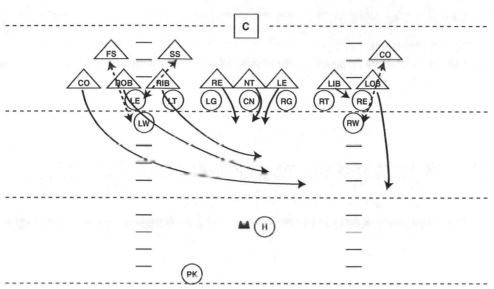

1. Both the kicking and blocking teams line up in their proper positions.
2. The three interior linemen, the RIB and ROB, and the right CO on the block team line up in a 3-point stance looking at the ball. The left IB and OB may also be in a 3-point stance, but they will not be involved in the rush.
3. On the snap, the two ends and NT rush up the center with the RIB rushing between the LE and LT, the ROB rushing between the LE and LW, and the right CO rushing just outside of the LW.
4. One team attempts to block three kicks, then a new group comes in and repeats the drill.
5. Usually it is best to have the outside rush come from the wide side of the field, so you can reverse the assignments when setting up a rush left block.

Coaching Points

- In the beginning of the year, have only the three outside rushers do the drill until they are taking the correct path and aiming for the correct spot to block the kick.
- Check that all six rushers move on the snap of the ball.
- The two ends direct their charge through the inside shoulder of each offensive guard, and the NT directs his charge through the shoulder of the CN on the wide side of the field.
- These three players need to drive hard for three steps, then extend their arms and try to jump in the air to deflect the ball.
- The RIB charges through the gap between the tackle and end, penetrating to a spot 2 yards in front of the tee to make the block.
- The ROB needs to penetrate between the end and the wing, staying as close to the end as possible. He also needs to anticipate the end blocking the IB.
- The right CO must drive to the outside hip of the wing. He needs to anticipate that the wing will

block the backer. Once he clears the wing, he can level out and aim for a spot 2 yards in front of the kicking tee.

- For safety, have the players coming from the outside extend and cross their arms in front of their face any time they are blocking the kick.
- The FS covers the LW and the SS covers the LE until the ball is kicked.
- The LIB steps forward, hits the RE and stays with him until the ball is kicked, while the left CO focuses on and covers the RW until the ball is kicked.
- The LOB rushes outside of the RW, comes up the field 5 yards and prepares to tackle the ball carrier, if the ball is not kicked, or recover the ball when it is blocked.
- Alert the members of the block team that if the ball is blocked and does not cross the line of scrimmage, they can pick it up and run for a touchdown.
- Emphasize to all the players on the block team that if the field goal is short, they do not have to recover the ball. They can allow it to roll dead, and it will still be their ball.
- Remind all rushers that they must avoid touching the PK as they make their rush.

PERIOD 5
Team Practice

Offensive Plays for Team Practice

In this section of the book we are focusing on running a wing-T formation, and the plays are examples of the types of plays that you may want to incorporate in your offensive team practice. Obviously if you use a different formation, you would use the plays that you feel are appropriate for the situation.

During this practice time the offensive plays that you run as an entire team can be organized by the plays that you might select to run in different down and distance situations:

- 1st and 10
- 2nd down
- 3rd down
- Short yardage and goal line

Using this type of organization during team period you can be certain that you have practiced plays that you will use in the game regardless of the down and distance situation.

🏈 1ST AND TEN SAMPLE PLAYS

Number of players: Full offense and defense
Equipment: Shorts or full pads, markers, ball
Time: 10 minutes/3 times a week

25 Lead

The following 1st and ten plays feature a far wing left formation, meaning that the halfback lines up on the opposite side of the line from the wing-back.

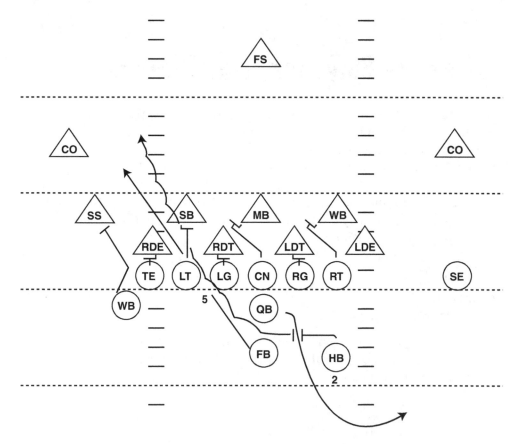

The 25 Lead is so named because the halfback (2 back) runs inside left tackle (the 5th hole). The diagram shows blocking assignments.

Fake 34 Lead

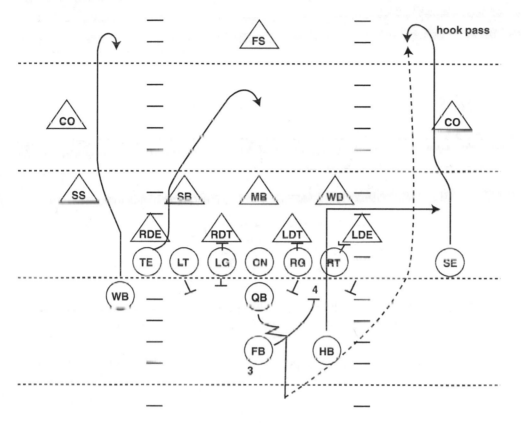

In the Fake 34 Lead, the quarterback fakes a handoff to the fullback (3 back), who fakes a run inside right tackle (the 4th hole). The quarterback then drops back to pass, here completing a hook pass to the split end.

34 Lead

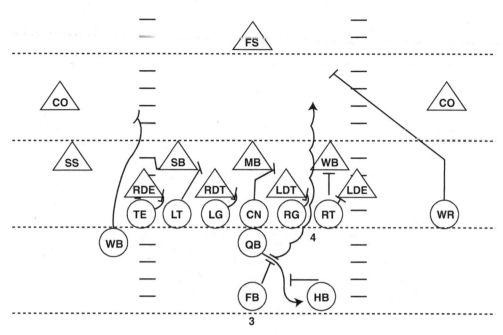

In the 34 Lead, the fullback takes the handoff and runs inside right tackle (4 hole).

SECOND DOWN SAMPLE PLAYS

For these 2nd down plays we remain in a far wing left formation.

29 Sweep

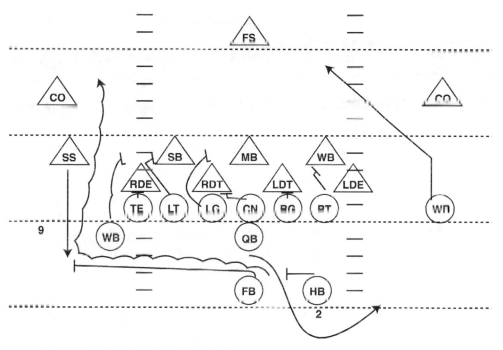

Here the halfback (2 back) takes the handoff and runs wide left (9 hole).
Note the blocking assignments.

Fake 29 Sweep

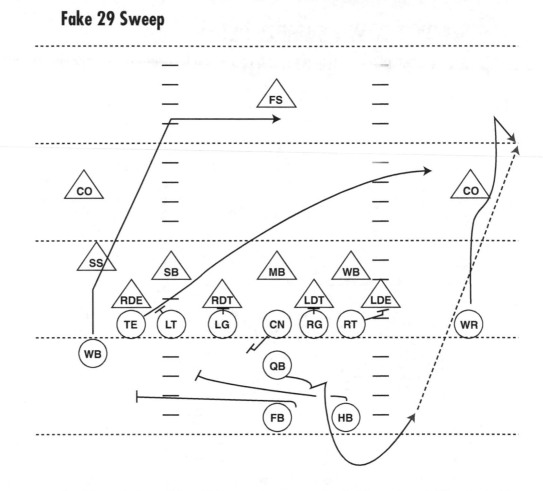

In this variation of the 29 Sweep the quarterback fakes a handoff to the halfback and then bootlegs right, with an option to run or pass. As drawn here, the QB passes to the wide recevier.

🏈 THIRD DOWN SAMPLE PLAYS

We'll show two possible plays for third and long, and two plays for third down and short or medium yardage.

In Pass—FLK and SE in routes, TE post and backs flat.

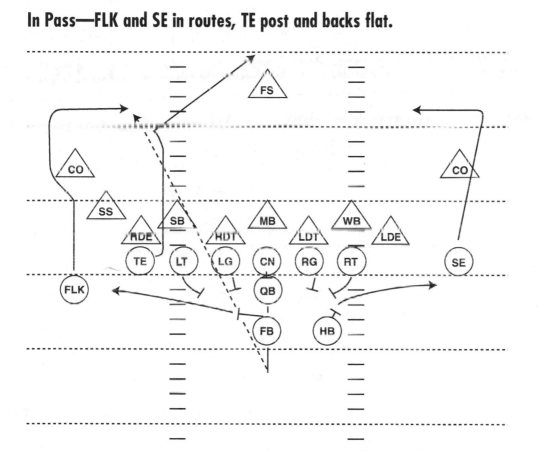

Third down and seven or more is an obvious passing situation. This pass play uses a far left formation in which the wingback splits out from the tight end and is therefore called a flanker. Here the tight end runs a post pattern, the flanker and split end run in routes, and the backs run flat patterns after blocking.

FB Screen Right

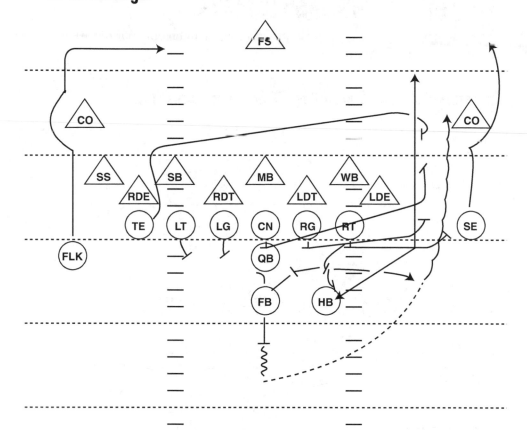

Anytime your offensive team is faced with a third and long situation, over 7 yards, you must anticipate that the defense may try to put a great deal of pressure on your quarterback by blitzing one or more linebackers or by dropping deep in a zone defense. When facing either of these two situations, throwing a screen pass to one of your backs can allow you to make the first down.

This play uses the same formation as the previous pass play, but the quarterback screens right to the fullback. The right end of the line pulls right to block, the tight end runs from left to right to block in the secondary, and the halfback leads the fullback downfield, ready to block any defender.

27 Power

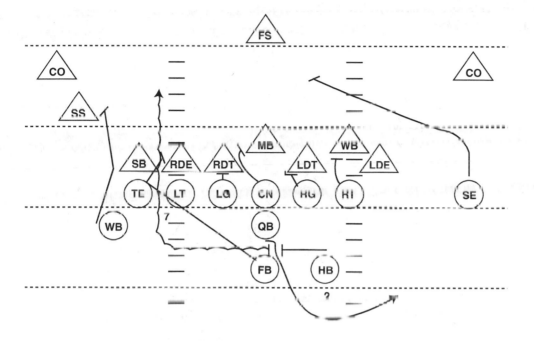

When you need 6 or fewer yards on third down, you have more options. In this play the halfback (2 back) takes the handoff and runs off left tackle (7 hole). The left tackle and tight end double-team block the right defensive end, the fullback blocks the strong-side linebacker, and the wingback blocks the strong safety.

Slant Pass

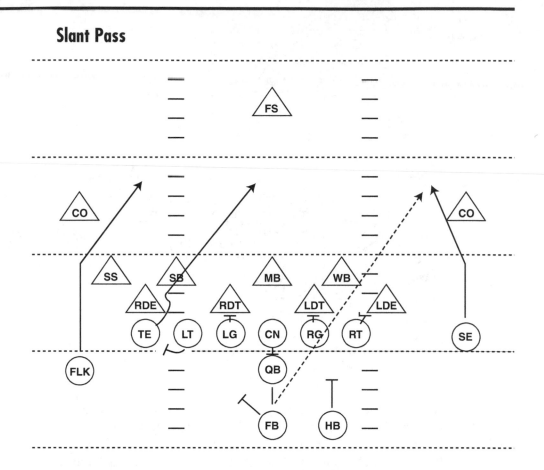

In this 3rd-and-6-or-less play we've split out the wingback again. Both he (now called the flanker) and the split end run 6-yard slant routes, and here the pass goes to the split end.

🏈 SHORT YARDAGE AND GOAL LINE SAMPLE PLAYS

The following are plays you can use coming out from your own goal line, on short yardage situations (3rd and 2 or less) out on the field, or at your opponent's goal line when you are trying to score.

The reason for using the second tight end is to have an additional blocker who can stop an outside rush man from tackling your ball carrier in the backfield, especially if the ball carrier is running to the other side of the formation. The second tight end also allows you to have greater strength running to both sides of your formation and can create doubt in the defense's mind as to where you are going to attack.

34 Slant

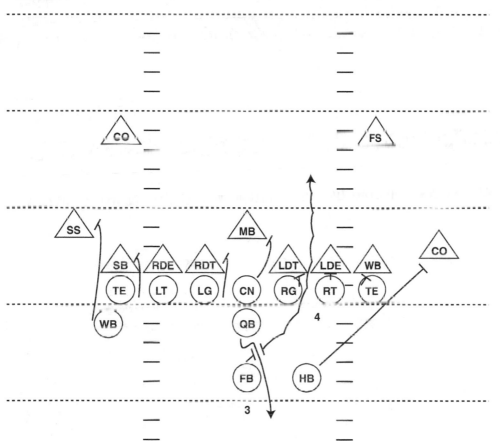

In this play the fullback (3 back) runs inside right tackle (the 4 hole). This is *power running*. Note that we're in a "far left wing tight" formation, meaning that the wingback lines up close to the tight end.

Nevertheless, when the defense is moving everyone up to the line of scrimmage to stop your running game, you may be forced to throw the ball. One option would be to throw a short, quick pass like the slant pass that we diagrammed earlier in this chapter. There are several advantages to using this type of pass:

- It is easier to complete
- You have less chance for an interception
- You can block all the rush men
- The quarterback has a much lower chance of being sacked

Another option is the following play.

Roll Out Right

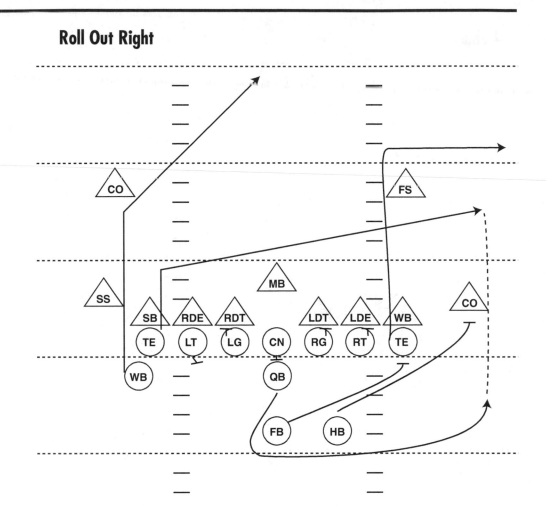

Here, by design, we move the quarterback to the outside, away from the rush. Once he is in this position, he has the option of running or passing the ball. Often if you only have 1 yard, he will be able to drive for the yardage. Here we gain 6 yards plus whatever the tight end can eke out after the catch.

29 Power

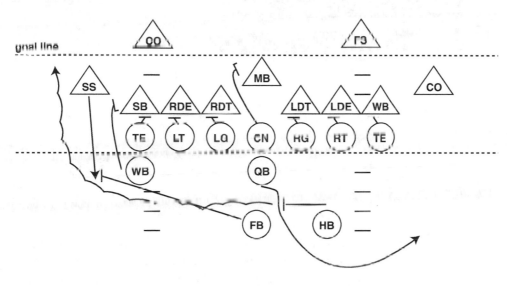

This sample is for a play near the goal line where all six defensive line play-ers charge hard from the line through their inside gaps. The WB looks for the SB or drives deep on the CO if he is not needed to double-team block the linebacker. Then instead of running between the TE and LT, the half-back runs the ball just outside the tight end.

Defensive Plays for Team Practice

In this chapter we are focusing on running a 4 - 3 (four linemen and three linebackers) or a 3 - 4 (three linemen, four linebackers) defense. Either combination gives you a seven-man front. Obviously if you use a different front, you would use the plays that you feel are appropriate for the situation. Many youth coaches like to feature an eight- or nine-man front to stop the run. This is easily achieved by adding one or two defensive backs to your 4 - 3 or 3 - 4 front, based on the coverage called. You can easily move the defensive backs up near the line of scrimmage and have them play as a linebackers, creating a strong run defense. You can then have the defensive backs move off the line of scrimmage and be in a better location to play the pass. Your front play and your pass coverage will be the same, and only the location of one or more of the defensive backs will have to be adjusted.

With this defensive organization, you'll be prepared to face older teams who throw the ball (and do it well). During defensive team period, it is best if you arrange your practice time so that you call the defenses that you anticipate using on different down and distance situations during the game:

- 1st and ten
- 2nd down
- 3rd down
- Short yardage and goal line

🏈 1ST AND TEN SAMPLE DEFENSES

Number of players: Full offense and defense
Equipment: Shorts or full pads, markers, ball
Time: 10 minutes/3 times a week

Base 4 - 3 Cover 2 (2-deep zone coverage)

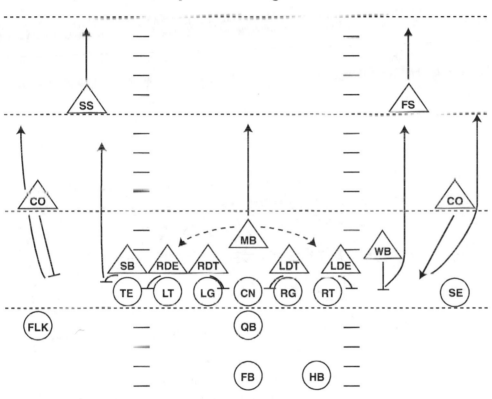

With this 4 - 3 defense, we are assigning each of our defensive linemen and outside linebackers to one gap. They know that they must be positioned in that gap if the offense tries to run in that area. The middle linebacker is assigned two gaps, one on either side, and must let the movement of the offensive backs tell him which way to go.

Cover two is a 2-deep coverage that allows both corners to come up if the offense tries to run wide to their side of the ball.

Keep in mind that the defensive options you have consist of:

1. A base front (3 - 4, 4 - 3, 5 - 2, 6 - 1, 6 - 2)
2. A complementary pass coverage (2-deep, 3-deep, 4-deep, man-to-man)
3. A dog package (where one LB rushes with zone or man-to-man coverage)

4. A full-out blitz package (where two or more LBs rush with man-to-man coverage)

3 - 4 Will Cover 2 (weak-side backer dog and 2-deep coverage)

With a 3 - 4 defense you have the luxury of blitzing with a weak-side line-

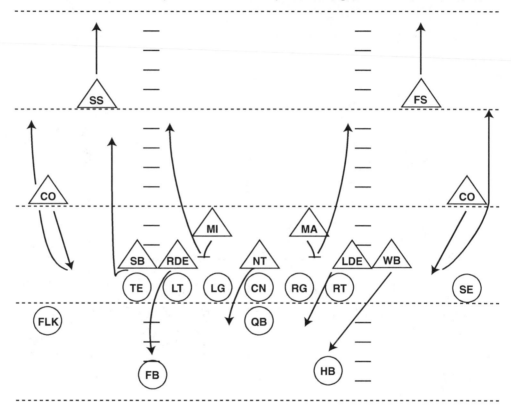

backer (WB), or Will, who can quickly get into the backfield and upset the timing of the play. In a 3 - 4 defense we use two inside linebackers. We differentiate the two by using the abbreviation MI, or Mike (the inside backer on the strong side of the formation) and MA, or Mac (the inside linebacker on the weak side of the formation). Both middle linebackers (MI and MA) need to use the movement of the offensive backs to tell them where to go. Our pass coverage can remain the same with the MA backer taking the place of the weak-side backer in our two-deep zone.

In our next defense, we will only have one defensive back (SS) who can quickly come to the line if the offense runs the ball to his side. Our other three defensive backs will be playing a deep third of the field and can only come up to help stop the run when the ball carrier crosses the line of scrimmage with the ball.

4 - 3 Lion Cover 3 (3-deep zone coverage)

In order to balance the defense and be in position to stop a run to both sides

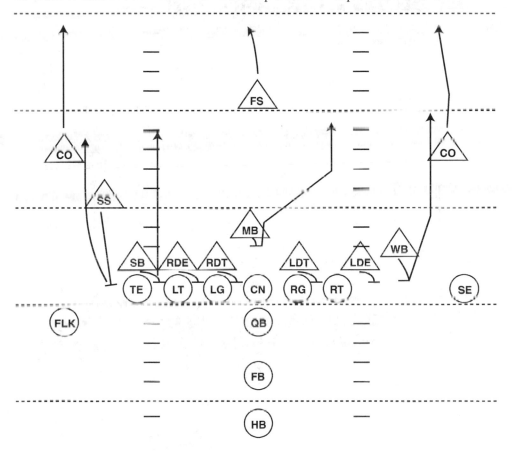

of the field, we have made a lion call, which tells the RDE, RDT, LDT, LDE, and WB that they have responsibility for the first gap on their left. We are now playing a 3-deep coverage with our two corners and the FS dividing up the field deep in thirds to stop any long pass.

🏈 SECOND DOWN SAMPLE DEFENSES

4 - 3 Ram Shoot Cover 2

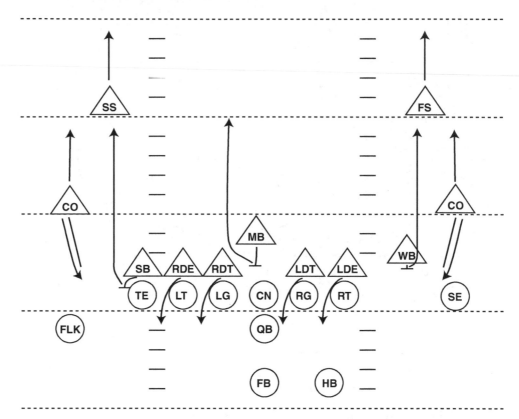

Here is a defensive call that tells the four defensive linemen they have gap responsibility to their right and they should penetrate across the line, or *shoot*. We will still play our 2-deep coverage, with both corners prepared to charge the line of scrimmage if the ball is run to their side. Cover two can also help stop any quick passes like the slant pass.

3 - 4 Mike Cover 1
(man-to-man pass coverage with a FS free in the middle)

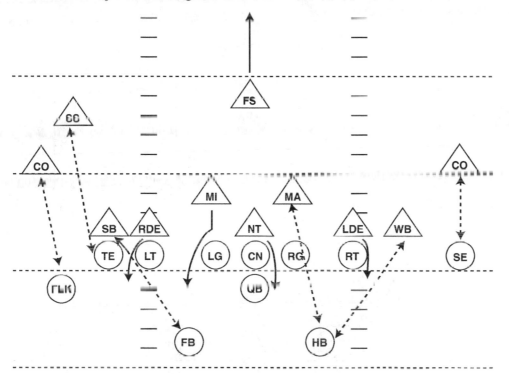

With our 3 - 4 defense, we can rush the MI over the LG on any running play and allow him to get penetration into the backfield.

We are now playing man-to-man pass defense that allows us to have tight coverage on the two wide receivers, tight end, and offensive backs, plus keeping the free safety free and deep in the middle of the field to key on the quarterback and go to the ball. When we run this style of defense, the nose tackle should take the center-guard gap on the opposite side from the MI backer.

🏈 THIRD DOWN SAMPLE DEFENSES

Anytime you are facing a third down situation, keep in mind that your objective should be to stop the offense from making a first down. If the offense needs 10 yards to make a first down and only makes 8, you have won. Stopping the offense, forcing them to punt, and turning the ball over to your offense should be the goal.

With this goal in mind, it is important to be very aware of the exact distance the offense needs to gain to make a first down and keep possession of the ball. When it is extremely long yardage, over 10 yards, you may elect to go to a defense that only rushes three defensive linemen and has the four linebackers and four defensive backs in coverage.

3 - 4 Cover 8 (4-deep zone coverage)

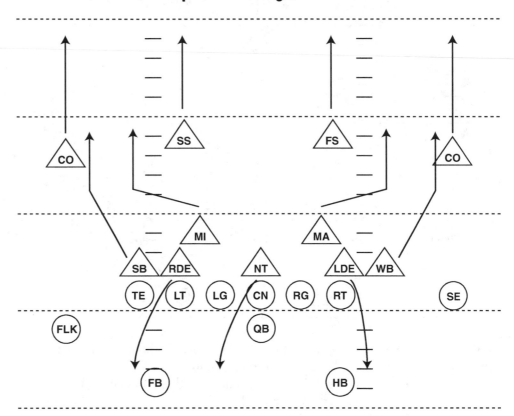

In our first third down sample defense, we have the offense in a long yardage situation, 3rd and 10 or more, and we want to protect against any extremely long pass play. To accomplish our objective we have elected to play cover 8, a coverage that allows all four defensive backs to drop deep and have responsibility for covering only one quarter of the field.

If the situation is in the 3rd and 4 or 5 range, we may decide that it is best to commit our defense to a blitzing situation where (1) we can put pressure on the quarterback before he is ready to pass the ball or (2) we have a good opportunity to tackle the ball carrier in the backfield before he can get started and reach the line of scrimmage.

4 - 3 SAW Cover Zero (man-to-man, no FS in the middle)

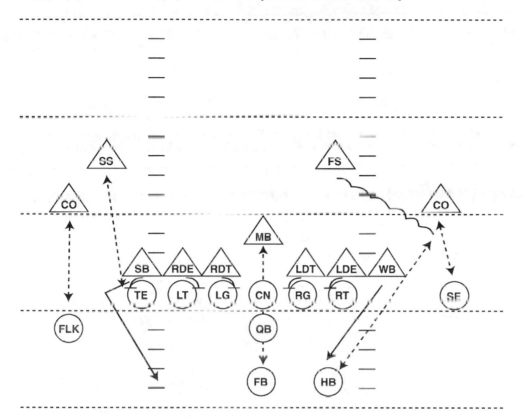

For a third down where the offense may only need 6 or 7 yards, we may feel that they are going to run, and consequently, we may elect to run a defense where we get penetration across the line of scrimmage and try to stop the play before it gets started. Now we will blitz our strong-side outside linebacker, or Sam, and weak-side outside linebacker, or Will (Sam + Will = SAW), across the line of scrimmage from the outside of each offensive tackle.

In cover zero, we will not have a defensive player free in the center of the field, so it is important that the two corners move to a position on the inside shoulder of the receiver they are covering, forcing any pass to go to the outside of the field. With this coverage, the FS has to move up to cover the HB if he comes out on a pass pattern.

If we face this same situation against a team that throws short to their outside receivers, we can have close cover 2 coverage, as in the following example.

3 - 4 Mac Cover 2 (MA backer dog and 2-deep coverage)

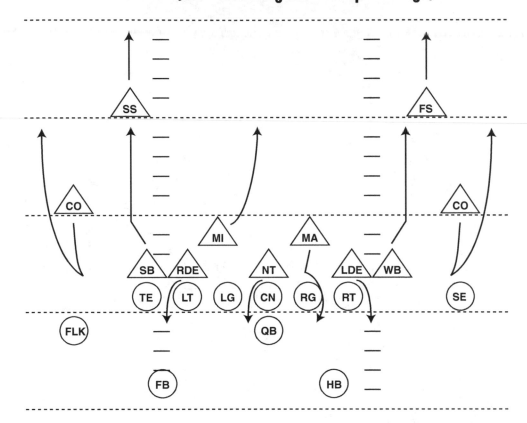

Here we rush our MA, or Mac, away from the TE to add pressure and get penetration across the line. We can maintain tight coverage on the two WRs and still have good support for the run without forcing us to go to an all-out blitz. Once again the nose tackle should take the gap away from the rushing linebacker.

🏈 SHORT YARDAGE AND GOAL LINE SAMPLE DEFENSES

Anytime your defense is in a short yardage situation, you want to stop the offense from making the first down, but you do not want to put your defense in a situation where the offense can get a big play on you.

Be very aware of the distance needed for the first down and whether or not the quarterback can gain the yardage by sneaking the ball. On a play that is third and one or two, you will need to defend the entire field. On a play that needs less than one yard, your emphasis will usually need to be on stopping a run somewhere between the offensive tackles.

4 - 3 SAW Cover 2 (SB and WB blitz with 2-deep coverage)

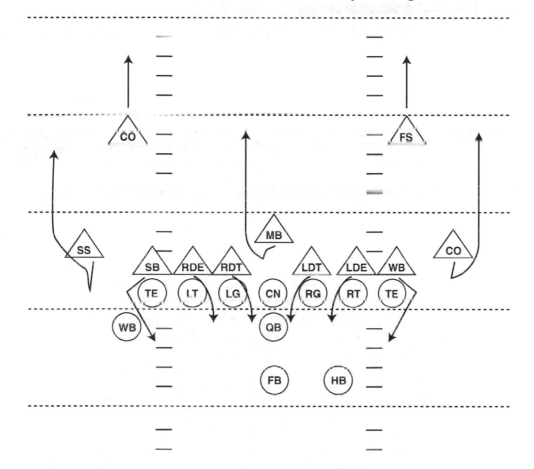

On the third and one or two, if the offense lines up with two tight ends and shrinks the formation, you have the luxury of blitzing your two outside linebackers and playing a safe 2-deep coverage.

If it is a pass play, the MB drops to the side of the movement by the offensive backs with the two COs dropping to underneath zone on their side.

4 - 3 SAW Pinch Cover Two (inside gap defense with SB and WB blitz and 2-deep coverage)

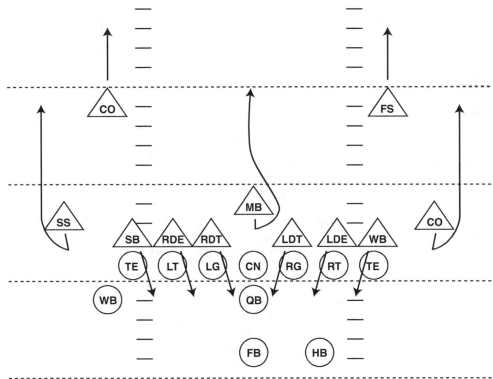

Once the distance needed by the offense is less than one yard, we need to quickly get a big body into all of the gaps on either side of the center. One easy way to accomplish this is to add a *pinch call* that tells the two outside linebackers and the four defensive linemen to charge hard through the first gap to their inside.

Two things happen when your opponent reaches your goal line area. First you must commit your players to stopping any gain by penetrating across the line, and second, your players need to understand there is only a limited amount of area that the offensive receivers can work in.

You may find that you will need to substitute in an extra linebacker if you feel that your free safety is not strong enough to fill the hole at the line and make the tackle.

You may also find that when the offense is 3 or 4 yards away from the goal line, you can easily use the same defense you use for short yardage and just move the defensive backs up closer to the line of scrimmage.

4 - 4 Gap SAW Cover Zero

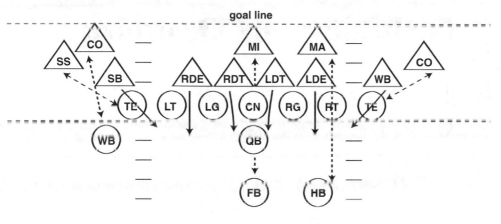

This is a 4 - 4 defense (four linemen, four linebackers) with the three defensive backs also crowding the line. The "gap" designation tells the two defensive tackles to move into the gaps either side of the center prior to the snap of the ball.

Near the goal line, it is very important that you coach the players with pass coverage responsibility to focus all their attention on the player they are assigned to cover. The strong corner has the WB, the SS has the TE on his side, the MI has the FB, the extra linebacker, the MA has the HB and the weak-side corner has the TE on his side. They must cover the receiver all over the field if he runs a pass route—they cannot be involved looking somewhere else and lose their pass coverage.

PERIOD 6
Cool-Down and Stretching

Wrapping Up

Now that you have finished the team period, it is time to bring the team back together, finish with offensive or defensive team movements, and end with a quick two-man buddy stretch.

With players playing both offense and defense, you may want to finish practice by running offensive plays one day and defensive plays at the end of practice the next day. If you can field an offensive and defensive team, you can run two drills at the same time.

On an offensive day, have the team huddle up, call a play, break the huddle, go to the line, and run the play with the entire team sprinting down the field for 15 yards.

If a pass play is called, the line holds at the line until the quarterback releases the ball, then sprint down the field.

For a defensive day, the defensive team huddles up, gets the defensive call, and lines up in the proper positions. One coach can be on a knee with the ball to simulate the center snap to start the drill. Another player with a ball can line up as a tailback and run wide to the right or left. The defensive players should execute their proper movements based on the defense called and take their pursuit angle to the ball carrier. Every defensive player needs to touch the ball carrier and continue up the field for 15 yards.

On a pass play, the rush men count to three, then rush at the man with the ball. The remaining players drop into their zones and turn to the ball when it is thrown. The rush men turn to the area of the pass, and once the interception is made, lead the ball carrier up the field for 15 yards.

During this time make certain that:

1. Every player gets a turn.
2. The players are onside and hustle during the entire play.
3. One group huddles up immediately after the first group has gone.

4. You give the team encouragement so that the players finish practice in a positive frame of mind.

For the stretch, match up your young players by size and weight. Have the players sit on the ground back to back. One player spreads his legs straight out in front of him, the width of his shoulders, with his knees flat on the ground. On your command of "Hut," the other player pushes up with both legs and rolls his back up on the back of his partner. This motion pushes his partner forward and stretches his legs. Then the players swap positions. Do a couple of stretches for each pair of players.

During this time try to have each coach visit with every player and offer praise for effort and performance so that the players are eager to return for the next session. They should also check on any injuries that might have occurred that day.

Try to have a brief coaches' meeting at the field once you have made certain that every player has been picked up and parents know about any injuries and suggested treatment. During this short meeting, discuss any areas that may need extra work and briefly discuss the next practice session.

As a coach you have a tremendous responsibility to your players and their parents. They are entrusting their children to your care. It is important that you do everything you can to honor this trust. Will you make mistakes? Of course you will—even veteran coaches make mistakes every season. The key is to learn from your mistakes and hopefully not repeat them. Be organized, keep your program simple, allow the players to play, tell your players what you want them to do, and always be as positive as you can. Every time you walk on the field for practice or a game, remember to:

1. Involve every player on the team.
2. Direct your attention and teaching to all of the players.
3. Strive to keep the players active.
4. Recognize effort and sportsmanship as well as athletic performance.
5. Never forget that the game is for the players first.
6. Tell the players why you are teaching them a skill so they develop a better understanding and appreciation of how the game is played.
7. Try to always remember that practice and games need to be fun for your entire team.

I salute each of you for taking on and accepting this challenge. I wish each of you good luck for this season and welcome you to the wonderful world of coaching football. From one coach to another, I sincerely hope that you have as much fun coaching your players as I've had with mine.

—Coach Tom Bass

Index

Numbers in **bold** refer to pages
with illustrations